Fix It!® Grammar

Robin Hood

STUDENT BOOK
LEVEL 3

Pamela White

Fourth Edition, January 2022
Institute for Excellence in Writing, L.L.C.

Copyright Policy
Fix It! Grammar: Robin Hood, Student Book Level 3
Fourth Edition version 4, January 2022
Copyright © 2022 Institute for Excellence in Writing

ISBN 978-1-62341-361-3

Our duplicating/copying policy for *Fix It! Grammar: Robin Hood*, Student Book Level 3:

All rights reserved.

No part of this book may be reproduced, stored in a retrieval system, or transmitted in any form or by any means, electronic, mechanical, photocopying, recording, or otherwise, without the prior written permission of the publisher, except as provided by U.S.A. copyright law and the specific policy below:

Home use: The purchaser may copy this Student Book for use by multiple children within his or her immediate family. Each family must purchase its own Student Book.

Small group or co-op classes: Each participating student or family is required to purchase a Student Book. A teacher may not copy from this Student Book.

Classroom teachers: A Student Book must be purchased for each participating student. A teacher may not copy from this Student Book.

Additional copies of this Student Book may be purchased from IEW.com/FIX-L3-S

Institute for Excellence in Writing (IEW®)
8799 N. 387 Road
Locust Grove, OK 74352
800.856.5815
info@IEW.com
IEW.com

Printed in Utah, United States of America

IEW®, Structure and Style®, and Fix It!® are registered trademarks of the Institute for Excellence in Writing, L.L.C.

Contributors
Sabrina Cardinale
Heidi Thomas
Denise Kelley

Designer
Melanie Anderson

Instructions

The list below shows the components to each *Fix It! Grammar* weekly exercise. Although **Mark It** is listed before **Fix It**, the student may choose to **Fix It** first and then **Mark It**. This is acceptable because the *Fix It! Grammar* exercises are like a word puzzle. The goal is to complete the lists at the top of the student page for each passage.

Students should discuss their work with the teacher after working through each daily passage. However, older students may work with their teacher on a weekly basis. Students should actively be involved in comparing their work with the Teacher's Manual. The repetition of finding and fixing their own mistakes allows them to recognize and avoid those mistakes in the future.

Fix It! Grammar should be treated as a game. Keep it fun!

Learn It!   On the first day of the new Week, read through the Learn It section. Each Learn It covers a concept that the student will practice in future passages. Instructions for marking and fixing passages are included in each Learn It.

Read It!   Read the day's passage.

Look up the bolded vocabulary word in a dictionary and pick the definition that fits the context of the story. Maintain a list of vocabulary words and their definitions.

The vocabulary definitions are printed in the Teacher's Manual.

Mark It!   Mark the passage using the guide at the top of the daily practice page.

Fix It!   Correct the passage using the guide at the top of the daily practice page.

The Teacher's Manual includes detailed explanations for grammar concepts and punctuation in each daily passage.

Rewrite It!   After marking, correcting, and discussing the passage with the teacher, copy the corrected passage on the lines provided or into a separate notebook.
- Copy the corrected story, not the editing marks.
- Indent and use capital letters properly.
- Copy the corrected punctuation.

Editing Marks

¶   indent

∧   insert

⌒   delete

≡   capitalize

/   lowercase

⌒   reverse order

add a space

⌒   close the space

Helpful Hints

Use different colors for **Mark It** and **Fix It**.

Appendix I Complete Story Familiarize yourself with the story that you will be editing by reading the complete story found in Appendix I.

Appendix II Collection Pages Look for strong verbs, quality adjectives, and -ly adverbs in this book and write them on the collection pages in Appendix II.

Appendix III Lists Refer to the lists found in Appendix III to quickly identify pronouns, prepositions, verbs, and conjunctions.

Appendix IV Grammar Glossary Reference the Grammar Glossary found in Appendix IV of the Teacher's Manual for more information about the concepts taught in the *Fix It! Grammar* series.

Additional Resource

Fix It! Grammar Cards are an optional product that will enhance the *Fix It! Grammar* learning experience.

Fix It! Grammar Cards

Thirty full color grammar cards highlight key *Fix It! Grammar* concepts for quick and easy reference.

For a more relaxed and entertaining way to drill and review grammar concepts learned, instructions for a download of multiple game ideas are included in the card pack.

Fix It! Grammar Cards are beautifully designed and come in a sturdy card box for easy storage.

IEW.com/FIX-GC

On the chart below *Fix It! Grammar Cards* are listed in the order that the information is taught in this book. Some cards are not introduced until future books.

WEEK	Fix It! Grammar Cards for *Robin Hood* Level 3
1	Editing Marks, Capitalization, Title, Noun, Pronoun, Preposition
2	Subject-Verb Pair, Verb, Linking Verb, Helping Verb, Conjunction, Coordinating Conjunction, Apostrophes
3	Adjective, Dependent Clause
5	Adverb
6	Sentence Openers, Prepositional Phrase
7	#3 -ly Adverb Opener, Number Words and Numerals
8	www Word
9	Indefinite Pronoun
10	Clause
11	Run-On
14	Interjection
15	Indentation, Quotation
25	Commas with Adjectives before a Noun
Not Used	#4 -ing Opener, Comparative and Superlative Adjectives and Adverbs

Scope and Sequence

Week numbers indicate when a concept is introduced or specifically reinforced in a lesson. Once introduced the concept is practiced throughout the book.

Week	1	2	3	4	5	6	7	8	9	10	11	12	13	14	15	16	17	18	19	20	21	22	23	24	25	26	27	28	29	30

Parts of Speech

	1	2	3	4	5	6	7	8	9	10	11	12	13	14	15	16	17	18	19	20	21	22	23	24	25	26	27	28	29	30
Noun	1			4							11																			
subject noun		2																												
noun of direct address					5																									
plural noun																			19											
Pronoun	1																													
personal pronoun	1																													
subject pronoun		2												14																
indefinite pronoun									9																					
demonstrative pronoun									9																					
reflexive pronoun																						22								
Preposition	1																			20										
prepositional phrase	1																17			20										
Verb																														
action verb		2		4			7				11																		29	
linking verb		2					7																						29	
helping verb		2					7																						29	
Coordinating Conjunction		2														16					21									
Adjective			3	4							11																			
article adj	1																													
possessive adj			3																19											
adj after linking verb			3																											
coordinate adjectives																									25					
cumulative adjectives																										26				
Adverb					5	6	7																							
Interjection														14																

Capitalization

	1	2	3	4	5	6	7	8	9	10	11	12	13	14	15	16	17	18	19	20	21	22	23	24	25	26	27	28	29	30
First Word of Sentence	1																													
Proper Noun	1																													
Personal Pronoun I	1																													
Interjection														14																
Quotation Marks															15															
Proper Adjective			3																											

Punctuation

	Week	1	2	3	4	5	6	7	8	9	10	11	12	13	14	15	16	17	18	19	20	21	22	23	24	25	26	27	28	29	30
End Marks																															
period	1																														
question mark	1																														
exclamation mark	1														14																
w/quotation marks																15															
Commas																															
a and b			2														16					21									
a, b, and c			2														16					21									
MC, cc MC																	16					21									
who/which clause				3																											
that clause					4																										
noun of direct address						5																									
#2 prepositional opener							6																								
#3 -ly adverb opener								7																							
adverb clause									8																						
#5 clausal opener												12																			
comma splice														13																	
interjection															14																
quotations																15															
coordinate adjectives																										25					
cumulative adjectives																											26				
Quotation Marks																	15													28		
Apostrophes																															
contraction			2																												
possessive adj																					19										

Clauses

	Week	1	2	3	4	5	6	7	8	9	10	11	12	13	14	15	16	17	18	19	20	21	22	23	24	25	26	27	28	29	30
Who/Which Clause				3							10	11												23							
That Clause					4						10																				
Adverb Clause									8		10		12								20										
Dependent Clause											10							17													
Main Clause											10							17													

Homophones/Usage

	Week	1	2	3	4	5	6	7	8	9	10	11	12	13	14	15	16	17	18	19	20	21	22	23	24	25	26	27	28	29	30
To/Two/Too					4																										
Its/It's						5																									
Your/You're						5																									
There/Their/They're										9																					
Whose/Who's															14																
Then/Than																			18												

Institute for Excellence in Writing *Fix It! Grammar: Robin Hood* Student Book Level 3

Other Concepts

	Week	1	2	3	4	5	6	7	8	9	10	11	12	13	14	15	16	17	18	19	20	21	22	23	24	25	26	27	28	29	30
Indentation		1														15															
Numbers								7																							
Subject-Verb Pairs			2																												
Fused Sentence												11		13																	
Comma Splice														13																	
Imperative Sentence															14																

Stylistic Techniques

	Week	1	2	3	4	5	6	7	8	9	10	11	12	13	14	15	16	17	18	19	20	21	22	23	24	25	26	27	28	29	30
Strong Verb			2																						24						
Quality Adjective				3																					24						
Who/Which Clause				3								11												23							
-ly Adverb						5								13											24						
Adverb Clause									8																						
#1 Subject Opener							6																								
#2 Prepositional Opener							6																					27			
#3 -ly Adverb Opener								7																							
#5 Clausal Opener													12															27			
#6 Vss Opener														13																	

Vocabulary

#	Words	#	Words	#	Words	#	Words	#	Words	#	Words
1	reigned, legendary, rambled, experienced	2	wrath, challenged, readily, strolled	3	entertaining, carefree, sociably, confronted	4	taunt, champion, exceptional, retorted	5	offense, composedly, seethed, capital	6	impulsively, furious, toppled, tortured
7	accounts, slain, vowed, lavish	8	sheltered, displaced, famished, narrowly	9	greedy, devastated, fled, peasants	10	declared, plundered, aid, earnestly	11	corrupt, courageous, peril, gurgling	12	romped, restless, directed, signal
13	roamed, spanned, stout, quickened	14	rudely, confident, riled, asserted	15	bellowed, lethal, crimson, sparring	16	countered, gazed, sturdy, fashioned	17	towered, rival, crafted, risk	18	goaded, victor, adept, nimbly
19	adversary, parried, leveled, deftly	20	budged, battled, fatigue, privately	21	delivered, recovered, inflamed, counterattacked	22	ridiculous, strutted, wield, echoed	23	rustled, steadfast, rugged, pounced	24	struggled, blameless, introduced, appoint
25	thrashing, motley, devoted, bout	26	instructed, paced, quiver, attentively	27	released, impressive, notched, flawlessly	28	magnificent, urged, extended, snickered	29	howled, jubilant, quipped, guffaw	30	retraced, festivity, warmly, trustworthy

Contents

Weekly Lessons

Week 1 1	Week 16 91
Week 2 7	Week 17 97
Week 3 13	Week 18 103
Week 4 19	Week 19 109
Week 5 25	Week 20 115
Week 6 31	Week 21 121
Week 7 37	Week 22 127
Week 8 43	Week 23 133
Week 9 49	Week 24 139
Week 10 55	Week 25 145
Week 11 61	Week 26 151
Week 12 67	Week 27 157
Week 13 73	Week 28 163
Week 14 79	Week 29 169
Week 15 85	Week 30 175

Appendices

Appendix I: Complete Story
　Robin Hood 185
Appendix II: Collection Pages
　-ly Adverb 191
　Strong Verb 193
　Quality Adjective 195
Appendix III: Lists
　Pronoun 197
　Preposition, Verb, Conjunction 198

Week 1

Learn It!

Every word belongs to a word group—a part of speech. There are eight parts of speech: noun, pronoun, verb, preposition, conjunction, adjective, adverb, interjection.

Noun

A **noun** names a person, place, thing, or idea.

A **compound noun** is two or more words combined to form a single noun. This includes proper nouns with two or more words, such as *King Richard*.

Article Adjective

The **article adjectives** are *a, an, the*. A noun follows an article adjective.

Pronoun

A **pronoun** replaces a noun in order to avoid repetition. It refers back to some person or thing recently mentioned and takes the place of that person or thing.

There are many types of pronouns. **Personal pronouns** take the place of common and proper nouns. Review the personal pronouns in Appendix III.

Preposition

A **preposition** starts a phrase that shows the relationship between a noun or pronoun and another word in the sentence. A prepositional phrase always begins with a preposition and ends with a noun or pronoun. Review the prepositions in Appendix III.

Memorize It! **preposition + noun (no verb)**

Mark It! Write *n* above each noun. Use a single *n* for a compound noun.
Write *ar* above each article and *pr* above each pronoun.
Underline each prepositional phrase.

        n   pr   n   ar   n
Robin Hood and his men lived <u>in the forest</u>.

---

8 Parts of Speech

Noun
Definition:
A noun names a person, place, thing, or idea.

Tests:
  the _____
  two _____

Pronoun
Definition:
A pronoun replaces a noun in order to avoid repetition.

List: Appendix III

Preposition
Definition:
A preposition starts a phrase that shows the relationship between a noun or pronoun and another word in the sentence.

Pattern:
preposition + noun (no verb)

List: Appendix III

Capitalization

Capitalize the first word of a sentence.

Capitalize proper nouns.

Capitalize the personal pronoun *I*.

>*Fix It!*   Place three short lines below letters that should be capitalized.

<u>r</u>obin lived in <u>s</u>herwood <u>f</u>orest. <u>h</u>e told his men, "<u>i</u> will hunt with you."

End Mark

Use a period at the end of a statement.

Use a question mark at the end of a question.

Use an exclamation mark at the end of a sentence that expresses strong emotion.

>*Fix It!*   Place the correct end mark at the end of each sentence.

Did Robin give up**?** He would never quit**!** He was used to challenges**.**

Indentation

Notice that some sentences are indented. An indented sentence means that the sentence begins a new paragraph.

>In fiction (stories), there are four reasons to start a new paragraph: new speaker, new topic, new place, new time.

Read It!	**Mark It!**	**Fix It!**	Week 1
			Day 1
1 vocabulary	2 articles (ar)	4 capitals	
	4 nouns (n)	1 end mark	
	3 prepositional phrases		

in the olden days of england, king richard

reigned over the land

Rewrite It! _____

_____

_____

_____

Read It!	**Mark It!**	**Fix It!**	Week 1
1 vocabulary	1 article (ar)	7 capitals	Day 2
	5 nouns (n)	1 end mark	
	1 pronoun (pr)		
	2 prepositional phrases		

a **legendary** outlaw lived in sherwood forest

in central england. his name was robin hood

Rewrite It! _____

Read It!	**Mark It!**	**Fix It!**	Week 1
			Day 3
1 vocabulary	3 articles (ar)	2 capitals	
	4 nouns (n)	1 end mark	
	2 pronouns (pr)		
	3 <u>prepositional phrases</u>		

robin and the loyal men with him **rambled** through

the countryside. they hunted in the deep forests

Rewrite It! _____

Read It!	Mark It!	Fix It!	Week 1
1 vocabulary	2 articles (ar)	3 capitals	Day 4
	5 nouns (n)	1 end mark	
	1 pronoun (pr)		
	3 prepositional phrases		

robin was skilled with the bow. in truth, he was the most **experienced** archer in england

Rewrite It! _____

Week 2

Learn It!

Verb

A **verb** shows action, links the subject to another word, or helps another verb. To determine if a word is a verb, use the verb test.

An **action verb** shows action or ownership.

A **linking verb** links the subject to a noun or adjective. The words below are linking verbs.

Memorize It!   am, is, are, was, were, be, being, been
seem, become, appear, grow, remain
taste, sound, smell, feel, look

A **helping verb** helps an action verb or a linking verb. The helping verb is always followed by another verb. The words below are helping verbs.

Memorize It!   am, is, are, was, were, be, being, been
have, has, had, do, does, did, may, might, must
can, will, shall, could, would, should

Every verb has a subject. The subject and verb (s v) belong together.

Subject

A **subject** is a noun or pronoun that performs a verb action. It tells who or what the clause is about.

Find It!   Read the sentence and look for the verb.
Ask, "Who or what ____ (verb)?"

Mark It!   Write *v* above each verb and *s* above each subject.

     s   v   v
Robin had practiced archery for many years.

    s   v
His skills were incredible.

Strong Verb

A **strong verb** dresses up writing because it creates a strong image or feeling. A strong verb is an action verb, never a linking or helping verb. Look for strong verbs in this book and write them on the Strong Verb collection page, Appendix II.

---

8 Parts of Speech

Verb

Definition:
A verb shows action, links the subject to another word, or helps another verb.

Verb Test:
I ____ .
It ____ .

Verb Lists:
Appendix III

8 Parts of Speech

Coordinating Conjunction

Definition:
A coordinating conjunction connects the same type of words, phrases, or clauses.

Acronym:
FANBOYS

Conjunction

A conjunction connects words, phrases, or clauses.

A **coordinating conjunction** connects the same type of words, phrases, or clauses.

Memorize It! F A N B O Y S
              for and nor but or yet so

Robin strolled through the forest and whistled happily.

Because the items that the cc connects must be grammatically the same, *and* connects two verbs, *strolled* and *whistled*. It does not connect the noun *forest* and the verb *whistled*.

Comma

A **comma** is used to separate items in a sentence. This week you will learn two comma rules.

✗ Do not use a comma before a coordinating conjunction when it connects two items in a series unless they are main clauses.
  PATTERN a and b

, Use commas to separate three or more items in a series.
  PATTERN a, b, and c

Mark It! Write *cc* above each coordinating conjunction.

Fix It!   Remove a comma before a coordinating conjunction that connects only two items in a series. Add commas to separate three or more items in a series.

✗ a and b

, a, b, and c

                    cc
Robin was brave, but reckless.

                              cc
He chose his arrow, pulled it back, and let it fly.

Contraction

A **contraction** combines two words into one. It uses an apostrophe to show where a letter or letters have been removed.

Fix It! Place an apostrophe to show where a letter or letters have been removed.

Robin decided that he shouldn't give up.

Week 2
Day 1

Read It!   **Mark It!**   **Fix It!**

1 vocabulary

4 articles (ar)
7 nouns (n)
1 pronoun (pr)
1 coordinating conjunction (cc)
3 prepositional phrases
2 subject-verb pairs (s v)

4 capitals
1 end mark
1 apostrophe

why was robin hood an outlaw under the **wrath** of the law? its an interesting story for children and adults

Rewrite It!

Week 2

Day 2

Read It!   **Mark It!**   **Fix It!**

Read It!	Mark It!	Fix It!
1 vocabulary	4 articles (ar)	2 capitals
	5 nouns (n)	1 comma
	1 coordinating conjunction (cc)	1 end mark
	2 prepositional phrases	
	1 subject-verb pair (s v)	

the sheriff of nottingham had **challenged** the local

archers to a shooting match, and even offered a prize

Rewrite It! _____

_____

_____

_____

10   Institute for Excellence in Writing *Fix It! Grammar: Robin Hood* Student Book Level 3

Read It!	Mark It!	Fix It!	
			Week 2
			Day 3
1 vocabulary	1 article (ar)	2 capitals	
	4 nouns (n)	2 commas	
	3 pronouns (pr)	1 end mark	
	1 coordinating conjunction (cc)		
	2 subject-verb pairs (s v)		

robin was just eighteen. he **readily** accepted the challenge grabbed his bow and left his hometown

Rewrite It! _____

Week 2

Day 4

Read It!	Mark It!	Fix It!
1 vocabulary	1 article (ar)	2 capitals
	3 nouns (n)	1 comma
	1 pronoun (pr)	1 end mark
	1 coordinating conjunction (cc)	1 apostrophe
	2 subject-verb pairs (s v)	

robin **strolled** merrily. the trip shouldnt take

him more than two, or three days

Rewrite It! _____

_____

_____

_____

_____

Week 3

Learn It!

Adjective

An **adjective** describes a noun or pronoun.

An adjective tells which one, what kind, how many, or whose.

Memorize It!   which one? what kind? how many? whose?

Robin crossed the slippery bridge.

An adjective usually comes before the word it describes. The adjective *slippery* describes *bridge*. What kind of bridge? *slippery*

The bridge appeared slippery.

An adjective may follow a linking verb. The linking verb (appeared) links the subject (bridge) to an adjective (slippery). The adjective *slippery* describes *bridge*. What kind of bridge? *slippery*

Robin carried his bow.

Because the possessive pronouns *my, your, his, her, its, our, their* function as adjectives, you will now mark them as adjectives. The pronoun *his* replaces *Robin's* and functions as an adjective. Whose bow? *his*

Find It!   Find the nouns and pronouns in the sentence.

Once you find a noun or pronoun, ask the adjective questions to identify the adjectives.

Mark It!   Write *adj* above each adjective.

                       adj   *adj*
Robin strolled through the quiet woods with his bow.
adj   *adj*
Robin's skill in archery was famous.

8 Parts of Speech

Adjective

Definition:
An adjective describes a noun or pronoun.

Test:
   the ___ pen

Questions:
   which one?
   what kind?
   how many?
   whose?

Capitalization

Capitalize proper adjectives formed from proper nouns.

The English flag flew at King Richard's castle.

The proper adjective *English* comes from the proper noun *England*, the name of a specific country. The proper adjective *King Richard's* comes from the proper noun *King Richard*, the name of a specific person.

Quality Adjective

A **quality adjective** dresses up writing because it creates a strong image or feeling. A quality adjective is more specific than a weak adjective. A weak adjective is overused, boring, or vague. Look for quality adjectives in this book and write them on the Quality Adjective collection page, Appendix II.

Dependent Clause

Who/Which Clause

Contains:
subject + verb

First Word:
who or which

Commas:
unless essential

Marking:
w/w

Who/Which Clause

A *who/which* clause is a group of words that describes the noun it follows. It begins with the word *who* or *which*, a relative pronoun.

Who refers to people, personified animals, and pets.
Which refers to things, animals, and places.

A *who/which* clause is a dependent clause, which means it must be added to a sentence that is already complete.

Robin eyed the target. *(sentence)*

Robin, who eyed the target. *(fragment)*

Robin, who eyed the target, picked up his bow. *(sentence)*

A *who/which* clause contains a subject and a verb. The subject of most *who/which* clauses is *who* or *which*, but sometimes the subject is another word in the clause.

Mark It! Place parentheses around the *who/which* clause and write *w/w* above the word *who* or *which*. Write *v* above each verb and *s* above each subject.

                                                                   s   v
                                     w/w
Robin thought about the contest, (which he hoped to win).

           s   v
   w/w
The men (who worked for the king) could not be trusted.

Comma

A **comma** is used to separate items in a sentence. Commas are used to separate the *who/which* clause from the rest of the sentence unless the *who/which* clause changes the meaning of the sentence.

, Place commas around the *who/which* clause if it is nonessential.

✗ Do not place commas around the *who/which* clause if it is essential (changes the meaning of the sentence).

When you rewrite the passages, copy the commas correctly.

Read It!	Mark It!	Fix It!	Week 3 Day 1
1 vocabulary	2 articles (ar)	2 capitals	
	3 nouns (n)	1 comma	
	1 pronoun (pr)	1 end mark	
	3 adjectives (adj)	1 apostrophe	
	1 coordinating conjunction (cc)		
	2 <u>prepositional phrases</u>		
	1 *who/which* clause (w/w)		
	3 subject-verb pairs (s v)		

robin whistled, and thought about the contest, which would be **entertaining**. he wasnt worried about the other archers

Rewrite It! _____

Week 3
Day 2

Read It!	**Mark It!**	**Fix It!**
1 vocabulary	1 article (ar)	3 capitals
	2 nouns (n)	1 end mark
	3 adjectives (adj)
	1 coordinating conjunction (cc)
	2 subject-verb pairs (s v)

the day seemed pleasant and **carefree**. however,

robin's mood would soon change

Rewrite It! _____

Read It!	Mark It!	Fix It!	Week 3
			Day 3
1 vocabulary	2 articles (ar)	2 capitals	
	4 nouns (n)	1 end mark	
	1 pronoun (pr)	1 comma	
	2 adjectives (adj)		
	1 coordinating conjunctions (cc)		
	2 <u>prepositional phrases</u>		
	1 *who/which* clause (w/w)		
	3 subject-verb pairs (s v)		

robin met fifteen foresters who worked for the king. they were sitting beneath a huge oak, and were feasting **sociably**

Rewrite It! _____

Week 3

Day 4

Read It!	Mark It!	Fix It!
1 vocabulary	2 articles (ar)	4 capitals
	6 nouns (n)	1 comma
	1 pronoun (pr)	1 end mark
	4 adjectives (adj)	
	2 coordinating conjunctions (cc)	
	1 <u>prepositional phrase</u>	
	1 *who/which* clause (w/w)	
	3 subject-verb pairs (s v)	

a man who had a scar on his face **confronted** robin.

he called robin's bow and arrows cheap, and shoddy

Rewrite It! _____

_____

_____

_____

_____

Week 4

Learn It!

That Clause

A ***that* clause** is a group of words that begins with the word *that* and contains a subject and a verb. A *that* clause is a dependent clause, which means it must be added to a sentence that is already complete.

Dependent **C**lause

***That* Clause**

Pattern:
that + subject + verb

Mark It! Place parentheses around the *that* clause and write ***that*** above the word *that*. Write ***v*** above each verb and ***s*** above each subject.

```
                    that   s      v              v
Robin knew (that he could win the contest).
```

First Word:
that

Comma

A **comma** is used to separate items in a sentence. Because *that* clauses are essential to the sentence, commas are not used with *that* clauses.

Commas:
none

✗ | *That* clauses do not take commas.

Marking:
that

Homophone

A **homophone** is a word that sounds like another word but is spelled differently and has a different meaning. Correctly use the homophones *to*, *two*, and *too*.

To is a preposition or part of an infinitive: *to Nottingham* (preposition);
                                                 to travel (infinitive).

Homophone

Two is a number: *two arrows* (2 arrows).

Too is an adverb meaning also or to an excessive degree: *traveled too; too excited*.

Fix It! Place a line through the incorrect homophone and write the correct word above it.

```
                  to              too                    two
Robin was headed ~~two~~ Nottingham ~~to~~. He brought his ~~to~~

straightest arrows.
```

Institute for Excellence in Writing *Fix It! Grammar: Robin Hood* Student Book Level 3   19

Think About It!

Many words can be used as different parts of speech. However, a word can perform only one part of speech at a time. For example, *light* can be a noun, adjective, or verb.

Noun: The light hurt my eyes.

> In this sentence *light* is a thing.
> A noun is a person, place, thing, or idea.

Adjective: The light rain was falling.

> In this sentence *light* describes rain. What kind of rain? *light*.
> An adjective describes a noun or pronoun.

Verb: The lamps light the room.

> In this sentence *light* is a verb. *Light* is the action. What *light* the room? *lamps*.
> The subject-verb pair is *lamps light*.

Read It!	Mark It!	Fix It!	Week 4 Day 1
1 vocabulary	4 nouns (n) 1 pronoun (pr) 6 adjectives (adj) 1 <u>prepositional phrase</u> 2 subject-verb pairs (s v)	3 capitals 1 end mark 1 homophone	

then robin grew angry. no young man likes other men too **taunt** him about his prize possessions

Rewrite It! _____

Read It!	Mark It!	Fix It!	Week 4
1 vocabulary	2 articles (ar)	3 capitals	Day 2
	6 nouns (n)	1 end mark	
	3 pronouns (pr)	1 homophone	
	4 adjectives (adj)		
	1 coordinating conjunction (cc)		
	4 <u>prepositional phrases</u>		
	1 *that* clause (that)		
	3 subject-verb pairs (s v)		

he boasted that he was as skillful with a bow and arrow as any man. he was headed too nottingham to prove his skill in a **champion** match

Rewrite It! _____

_____

_____

_____

Week 4
Day 3

Read It!

1 vocabulary

Mark It!

3 articles (ar)
5 nouns (n)
1 pronoun (pr)
4 adjectives (adj)
1 coordinating conjunction (cc)
3 prepositional phrases
1 *who/which* clause (w/w)
2 subject-verb pairs (s v)

Fix It!

1 capital
1 comma
1 end mark

he planned to shoot with other archers for the grand prize, which was a barrel of **exceptional** ale, and a new bow

Rewrite It!

Week 4
Day 4

Read It!	Mark It!	Fix It!
1 vocabulary	1 article (ar)	2 capitals
	5 nouns (n)	1 comma
	4 pronouns (pr)	1 end mark
	4 adjectives (adj)	
	1 coordinating conjunction (cc)	
	3 <u>prepositional phrases</u>	
	2 *that* clauses (that)	
	4 subject-verb pairs (s v)	

one forester laughed at him, and **retorted** that he had big words for a little boy! he said that he should drink his ale with milk

Rewrite It! _____

Learn It!

Adverb

An **adverb** modifies a verb, an adjective, or another adverb.

An adverb tells how, when, where, why, to what extent.

Memorize It!   how? when? where? why? to what extent?

An adverb often ends in -ly.

Mark It!   Write *adv* above each -ly adverb.

        adv
The deer carefully hid in a secluded thicket.

-ly Adverb

An **-ly adverb** dresses up writing when it creates a strong image or feeling. Look for -ly adverbs in this book and write them on the -ly Adverb collection page, Appendix II.

Noun of Direct Address

A **noun of direct address** (NDA) is a noun used to refer to someone directly. It names the person spoken to.

It can appear at any natural pause in a quoted sentence.

"Robin, tomorrow you will win the contest," his friend said.

"Tomorrow, Robin, you will win the contest," his friend said.

"Tomorrow you will win the contest, Robin," his friend said.

Because a noun can perform only one function in a sentence, a noun of direct address is never the subject of a sentence. In these sentences the noun of direct address is *Robin* because that is the noun used to directly address Robin. The subject is the pronoun *you*.

Comma

A **comma** is used to separate items in a sentence. Commas are used to separate the noun of direct address from the rest of the sentence.

Place commas around a noun of direct address.

Fix It!   Add commas to separate the noun of direct address from the sentence.

"Robin, you should enter the contest," his friend suggested.

---

8 Parts of Speech

Adverb

Definition:
An adverb modifies a verb, an adjective, or another adverb.

Questions:
how?
when?
where?
why?
to what extent?

Homophone

A **homophone** is a word that sounds like another word but is spelled differently and has a different meaning. Correctly use the homophones *its* and *it's, your* and *you're*.

Its is a possessive pronoun: *its target* (the target belongs to it).

The possessive pronoun *its* tells whose and functions as an adjective.

It's is a contraction: *it's spring* (it is spring).

The contraction *it's* is a shortened form of *it is* and functions as the subject pronoun (it) and verb (is) of the clause.

Your is a possessive pronoun: *your bow* (the bow belongs to you).

The possessive pronoun *your* tells whose and functions as an adjective.

You're is a contraction: *you're right* (you are right).

The contraction *you're* is a shortened form of *you are* and functions as the subject pronoun (you) and verb (are) of the clause.

Fix It! Place a line through the incorrect homophone and write the correct word above it.

It's **its**
~~Its~~ trying to hide, but ~~it's~~ antlers are showing.

You're **your**
~~Your~~ on ~~you're~~ way to the archery contest.

Read It!	Mark It!	Fix It!	Week 5
			Day 1

Read It!
1 vocabulary

Mark It!
4 articles (ar)
8 nouns (n)
5 pronouns (pr)
1 adjective (adj)
1 adverb (adv)
1 coordinating conjunction (cc)
2 prepositional phrases
1 *that* clause (that)
4 subject-verb pairs (s v)

Fix It!
4 capitals
2 commas
1 end mark

robin immediately took **offense**, and challenged the forester. "sir do you see the deer at the edge of the wood? i bet you twenty pounds that i can hit it"

Rewrite It! _____

Week 5
Day 2

Read It!	Mark It!	Fix It!
1 vocabulary	2 articles (ar)	2 capitals
	7 nouns (n)	2 commas
	4 adjectives (adj)	1 end mark
	1 adverb (adv)	1 homophone
	1 coordinating conjunction (cc)	
	3 <u>prepositional phrases</u>	
	1 subject-verb pair (s v)	

composedly robin took his bow in his hand grabbed an arrow from it's pouch and drew the feather to his ear

Rewrite It! _____

Read It!	Mark It!	Fix It!	Week 5 Day 3
1 vocabulary	5 articles (ar) 6 nouns (n) 1 adverb (adv) 1 <u>prepositional phrase</u> 1 *who/which* clause (w/w) 3 subject-verb pairs (s v)	2 capitals 1 end mark	

the arrow hit the buck. the foresters **seethed** with rage, especially the man who lost the bet

Rewrite It! _____

Week 5

Day 4

Read It!	Mark It!	Fix It!
1 vocabulary	3 articles (ar)	4 capitals
	5 nouns (n)	1 comma
	3 pronouns (pr)	1 end mark
	2 adjectives (adj)	2 homophones
	1 adverb (adv)	
	1 <u>prepositional phrase</u>	
	4 subject-verb pairs (s v)	

the loser heatedly responded, "fool you killed the king's deer. its a **capital** offense. by law your going to die"

Rewrite It! _____

Week 6

Learn It!

Sentence openers are descriptive words, phrases, and clauses that are added to the beginning of a sentence. Using different sentence openers makes writing more interesting.

In this book you will learn five types of sentence openers—five ways to open or begin a sentence. After you mark a sentence, determine if the sentence begins with an opener that you know. If it does, mark it! Do not mark questions or quoted sentences.

#1 Subject Opener

A **#1 subject opener** is a sentence that begins with the subject of the sentence. Sometimes, an article or adjective will come before the subject, but the sentence is still a #1 subject opener.

Mark It! Write ① above the first word of a sentence that starts with a subject opener.

① S   V
Robin spotted a deer in the field.

①   S   V
The swift deer leaped into the forest.

#2 Prepositional Opener

A **#2 prepositional opener** is a sentence that begins with a prepositional phrase. The first word in the sentence must be a preposition.

Mark It! Write ② above the first word of a sentence that starts with a prepositional phrase.

②
Along the road Robin walked quickly.

②
Along the narrow and winding road, Robin walked quickly.

②
Along the narrow and winding road toward Nottingham, Robin walked quickly.

Comma

A **comma** is used to separate items in a sentence.

, | If a prepositional opener has five words or more, follow it with a comma.

If two or more prepositional phrases open a sentence, follow the last phrase with a comma.

When you rewrite the passages, copy the commas correctly.

Institute for Excellence in Writing *Fix It! Grammar: Robin Hood* Student Book Level 3   31

Adverb

An **adverb** modifies a verb, an adjective, or another adverb.

An adverb tells how, when, where, why, to what extent.

Week 5 you learned that an adverb often ends in *-ly*. However, many adverbs do not end in *-ly*. Some common examples include *very, together, never, soon*.

Robin usually had his bow with him.

An adverb often ends in *-ly*.
The adverb *usually* tells when.

Robin always had his bow with him.

Some adverbs do not end in *-ly*.
The adverb *always* tells when.

Robin did not have his bow with him.

The words *yes, no, not, too* function as adverbs.
When you see them, label them adverbs.

Mark It!   Write *adv* above each adverb

                          adv   *adv*
Robin was very confident as he carefully aimed at the deer.

Read It!	Mark It!	Fix It!	Week 6
			Day 1

Read It!

1 vocabulary

Mark It!

2 articles (ar)
6 nouns (n)
2 adjectives (adj)
1 adverb (adv)
1 coordinating conjunction (cc)
3 <u>prepositional phrases</u>
1 subject-verb pair (s v)
1 opener

Fix It!

2 capitals
2 commas
1 end mark

in anger the forester **impulsively** sprang to his feet grabbed his bow and shot an arrow at robin

Rewrite It! _____

Week 6
Day 2

Read It!	Mark It!	Fix It!
1 vocabulary	3 articles (ar)	3 capitals
	5 nouns (n)	1 end mark
	1 pronoun (pr)	
	3 adjectives (adj)	
	1 adverb (adv)	
	2 <u>prepositional phrases</u>	
	1 *that* clause (that)	
	3 subject-verb pairs (s v)	
	2 openers	

robin hood was fortunate that the arrow barely missed him. without delay the **furious** forester reached for a second arrow

Rewrite It! _____

Read It!	Mark It!	Fix It!	Week 6
			Day 3
1 vocabulary	3 articles (ar)	3 capitals	
	5 nouns (n)	1 end mark	
	1 pronoun (pr)		
	1 adjective (adj)		
	1 adverb (adv)		
	2 <u>prepositional phrases</u>		
	1 *who/which* clause (w/w)		
	3 subject-verb pairs (s v)		
	2 openers		

in self-defense young robin shot an arrow, which struck the man. he **toppled** forward with a cry

Rewrite It!

Week 6

Day 4

Read It!	**Mark It!**	**Fix It!**
1 vocabulary	1 article (ar)	3 capitals
	3 nouns (n)	1 end mark
	2 pronouns (pr)	1 apostrophe
	2 adjectives (adj)
	1 adverb (adv)
	1 *that* clause (that)
	3 subject-verb pairs (s v)
	2 openers

robin hood was very upset. it **tortured** his conscience that hed killed a man

Rewrite It! _____

_____

_____

_____

_____

Learn It!

#3 -ly Adverb Opener

A **#3 -ly adverb opener** is a sentence that begins with an -ly adverb.

Mark It!   Write ③ above the first word of a sentence that starts with an -ly adverb.

③ -ly
Surprisingly, Robin approached the town.

③ -ly
Confidently Robin approached the town.

Comma

A **comma** is used to separate items in a sentence. A comma is used to separate an -ly adverb opener from the rest of the sentence when the -ly adverb modifies the sentence.

, | Use a comma if an -ly adverb opener modifies the sentence.

✗ | Do not use a comma if an -ly adverb opener modifies the verb.

When you rewrite the passages, copy the commas correctly.

Numbers

Spell out numbers that can be expressed in one or two words, like *twelve* and *one hundred*.

Use a hyphen with numbers from twenty-one to ninety-nine.

Spell out ordinal numbers, like *first* and *second*.

Ordinal numbers tell the order or position in a sequence.

Fix It!   Place a line through the incorrect number and write the correct word above it.

nine
Robin had 9̶ arrows in his quiver.

Think About It!

According to the verb definition, there are three categories of verbs: action, linking, helping. Every clause has an action verb or a linking verb. When a helping verb helps either an action verb or a linking verb, the two verbs together are called the verb phrase.

Action: Robin shot an arrow.

> In this sentence *shot* is the action verb. *Shot* is the action that Robin is doing.

Linking: Robin felt upset.

> In this sentence *felt* is the linking verb. *Felt* links the subject *Robin* to the adjective *upset*.

Helping + Action: Robin had shot an arrow.

> In this sentence *had* is a helping verb helping the action verb *shot*. *Had shot* is the verb phrase.

Helping + Linking: Robin did feel upset.

> In this sentence *did* is a helping verb helping the linking verb *feel*. *Did feel* is the verb phrase.

Linking Verbs List
---

    am, is, are, was, were, be, being, been (be verbs)

    seem, become, appear, grow, remain

    taste, sound, smell, feel, look (verbs dealing with the senses)

Helping Verbs List
---

    am, is, are, was, were, be, being, been (be verbs)

    have, has, had, do, does, did, may, might, must

    can, will, shall, could, would, should

Week 7
Day 1

Read It! **Mark It!** **Fix It!**

1 vocabulary
1 article (ar)
4 nouns (n)
1 pronoun (pr)
1 adjective (adj)
3 adverbs (adv)
1 coordinating conjunction (cc)
2 prepositional phrases
2 subject-verb pairs (s v)
2 openers

6 capitals
1 end mark
1 comma
1 number

fearfully robin hood escaped to sherwood forest.

he was an outlaw on 2 **accounts**, and could not

return home

Rewrite It! _____

_____
_____
_____

Week 7

Day 2

Read It!	Mark It!	Fix It!
1 vocabulary	4 articles (ar)	1 capital
	5 nouns (n)	1 comma
	1 pronoun (pr)	1 end mark
	3 adjectives (adj)	1 homophone
	1 adverb (adv)	
	1 coordinating conjunction (cc)	
	2 <u>prepositional phrases</u>	
	1 *that* clause (that)	
	2 subject-verb pairs (s v)	
	1 opener	

in a single day he had shot a deer that the king reserved for his own table, and had **slain** a man to

Rewrite It! _____

_____

_____

_____

_____

Read It!

1 vocabulary

Mark It!

2 articles (ar)
4 nouns (n)
1 pronoun (pr)
2 adjectives (adj)
1 adverb (adv)
1 coordinating conjunction (cc)
1 prepositional phrase
1 *that* clause (that)
3 subject-verb pairs (s v)
2 openers

Fix It!

4 capitals
1 end mark

Week 7
Day 3

the sheriff of nottingham and the dead forester were related. firmly he **vowed** that robin must be punished

Rewrite It! _____

Week 7

Day 4

Read It!
1 vocabulary

Mark It!
3 articles (ar)
5 nouns (n)
1 pronoun (pr)
3 adjectives (adj)
3 prepositional phrases
1 *who/which* clause (w/w)
1 *that* clause (that)
3 subject-verb pairs (s v)
1 opener

Fix It!
2 capitals
1 end mark
1 homophone
1 number

within a few days robin heard that a **lavish** reward of 200 pounds would be given two the man who captured him

Rewrite It! _____

_____

_____

_____

_____

Learn It!

Adverb Clause

An **adverb clause** is a group of words that begins with a www word and contains a subject and a verb. An adverb clause is a dependent clause, which means it must be added to a sentence that is already complete.

Memorize It!   **www word + subject + verb**

Use the acronym *www.asia.b* to remember the eight most common www words.

Memorize It!

w	w	w	a	s	i	a	b
when	while	where	as	since	if	although	because

Mark It!   Place parentheses around the adverb clause and write *AC* above the www word. Write *v* above each verb and *s* above each subject.

   AC   s   v
(Because Robin was now an outlaw), he had to hide
   AC   s   v   v
(where the sheriff could not find him).

Dependent Clause

Adverb Clause

Pattern:
www word + subject + verb

First Word:
www word

Commas:
after, not before

Marking:
AC

Comma

A **comma** is used to separate items in a sentence. A comma is used after but not before an adverb clause.

> **,** Use a comma after an adverb clause that comes before a main clause.
> **PATTERN AC, MC**

> **✗** Do not use a comma before an adverb clause.
> **PATTERN MC AC**

When you rewrite the passages, copy the commas correctly.

Think About It!

Many words can be used as different parts of speech. However, a word can perform only one part of speech at a time. For example, *as* can be a preposition that begins a prepositional phrase, and *as* can be a www word that begins an adverb clause.

    Prepositional Phrase: <u>As an outlaw</u> Robin hid from the sheriff.

       As an outlaw is a prepositional phrase.
       PATTERN preposition (As) + noun (outlaw) (no verb)

    Adverb Clause: (As he hid in the forest), Robin collected a band of loyal men.

       As he hid in the forest is an adverb clause.
       PATTERN www word (As) + subject (he) + verb (hid)

Read It!   **Mark It!**   **Fix It!**

Week 8, Day 1

- 1 vocabulary
- 1 article (ar)
- 5 nouns (n)
- 1 pronoun (pr)
- 4 adjectives (adj)
- 1 coordinating conjunction (cc)
- 2 prepositional phrases
- 1 adverb clause (AC)
- 2 subject-verb pairs (s v)
- 1 opener
- 4 capitals
- 1 comma
- 1 end mark

for an entire year robin **sheltered** in sherwood forest while he met other outlaws, and gained valuable hunting skills

Rewrite It!

Week 8
Day 2

Read It!
1 vocabulary

Mark It!
1 article (ar)
4 nouns (n)
1 pronoun (pr)
4 adjectives (adj)
1 adverb (adv)
2 prepositional phrases
2 subject-verb pairs (s v)
2 openers

Fix It!
2 capitals
1 end mark

eventually, he gathered a band of loyal men. these good men had been **displaced** for many reasons

Rewrite It!

Read It!	**Mark It!**	**Fix It!**	Week 8
			Day 3
1 vocabulary	3 nouns (n)	1 capital	
	1 pronoun (pr)	1 end mark	
	3 adjectives (adj)	1 homophone	
	1 adverb (adv)		
	1 *who/which* clause (w/w)		
	1 adverb clause (AC)		
	3 subject-verb pairs (s v)		
	1 opener		

some men, who were **famished**, shot deer because they had to little food

Rewrite It! _____

Read It!	Mark It!	Fix It!
1 vocabulary	2 articles (ar)	1 capital
	2 nouns (n)	1 end mark
	2 pronouns (pr)	1 apostrophe
	1 adjective (adj)	
	1 adverb (adv)	
	1 <u>prepositional phrase</u>	
	1 adverb clause (AC)	
	2 subject-verb pairs (s v)	
	1 opener	

Week 8
Day 4

theyd **narrowly** escaped from the foresters when they were hunting the king's deer

Rewrite It! _____

Learn It!

Pronoun

A **pronoun** replaces a noun in order to avoid repetition.

There are many types of pronouns. Week 1 you reviewed **personal pronouns**, which take the place of common and proper nouns.

An **indefinite pronoun** is not definite. It does not refer to any particular person or thing. The words below are indefinite pronouns.

all	both	few	one	own
another	each	many	other	several
any	either	more	others	some
anybody	everybody	most	nobody	somebody
anyone	everyone	much	no one	someone
anything	everything	neither	nothing	something
anywhere	everywhere	none	nowhere	somewhere

A **demonstrative pronoun** points to a particular person or thing. There are only four demonstrative pronouns.

this   that   these   those

Mark It!   Write *pr* above each pronoun.

  pr   *pr*   *pr*
Many had nowhere to go. That was tragic!

Think About It!

Many words can be used as different parts of speech. However, a word can perform only one part of speech at a time. The indefinite and demonstrative pronouns function as pronouns when they take the place of a noun. However, these same words function as adjectives when they come before a noun.

Pronoun: Many had nowhere to go.

In this sentence *Many* is a pronoun because it takes the place of the names of the people who had nowhere to go. *Many* is the subject of the clause.

Adjective: Many families had nowhere to go.

In this sentence *Many* is an adjective because it comes before a noun and tells how many families.

Pronoun: That was tragic.

In this sentence *That* is a pronoun because it takes the place of the explanation of what was tragic. *That* is the subject of the clause.

Adjective: That arrow hit the target.

In this sentence *That* is an adjective because it comes before a noun and tells which arrow.

That Clause: Robin knew (that the poor families needed help).

In this sentence *that* is used to begin a dependent clause. It is followed by a subject and a verb and completes the main clause telling what Robin knew.

Homophone

A **homophone** is a word that sounds like another word but is spelled differently and has a different meaning. Correctly use the homophones *there*, *their*, and *they're*.

There is an adverb pointing to a place: *over there* (there is the spot).

Their is a possessive pronoun: *their arrows* (the arrows belong to them).

The possessive pronoun *their* tells whose and functions as an adjective.

They're is a contraction: *they're angry* (they are angry).

The contraction *they're* is a shortened form of *they are* and functions as the subject pronoun (they) and verb (are) of the clause.

Fix It! Place a line through the incorrect homophone and write the correct word above it.

The archers raised ~~there~~ *their* bows to shoot the target over ~~their~~ *there*.

Week 9
Day 1

Read It!	**Mark It!**	**Fix It!**

1 vocabulary

Mark It!
- 1 article (ar)
- 3 nouns (n)
- 1 pronoun (pr)
- 5 adjectives (adj)
- 1 coordinating conjunction (cc)
- 1 *who/which* clause (w/w)
- 1 adverb clause (AC)
- 3 subject-verb pairs (s v)
- 1 opener

Fix It!
- 1 capital
- 1 comma
- 1 end mark
- 2 homophones

others, who were strong, and goodhearted, had lost they're farms because the **greedy** king wanted there lands

Rewrite It! _____

_____

_____

_____

Week 9

Day 2

Read It!	**Mark It!**	**Fix It!**
1 vocabulary	1 noun (n)	1 capital
	2 pronouns (pr)	1 end mark
	1 adjective (adj)	1 apostrophe
	2 adverbs (adv)	
	1 <u>prepositional phrase</u>	
	1 *that* clause (that)	
	2 subject-verb pairs (s v)	
	1 opener	

tragically, some had been **devastated** by unreasonable taxes that they couldnt pay

Rewrite It! _____

Read It!	Mark It!	Fix It!	Week 9
			Day 3
1 vocabulary	4 nouns (n)	4 capitals	
	2 adjectives (adj)	1 comma	
	1 adverb (adv)	1 end mark	
	1 coordinating conjunction (cc)	1 homophone	
	3 <u>prepositional phrases</u>		
	1 subject-verb pair (s v)		
	1 opener		

throughout england poor families **fled** from there homes, and secretly hid in sherwood forest

Rewrite It! _____

Week 9

Day 4

Read It!	Mark It!	Fix It!
1 vocabulary	1 article (ar)	3 capitals
	4 nouns (n)	1 end mark
	1 pronoun (pr)	1 homophone
	3 adjectives (adj)	1 number
	1 adverb (adv)	
	1 prepositional phrase	
	1 who/which clause (w/w)	
	2 subject-verb pairs (s v)	
	1 opener	

a band of 45 brave **peasants**, who greatly admired robin hood, chose him to be there leader

Rewrite It! _____

_____

_____

_____

_____

Learn It!

Clause
A **clause** is a group of related words that contains both a subject and a verb.

Dependent Clause
A **dependent clause** is a clause that cannot stand alone as a sentence because it does not express a complete thought. Dependent clauses begin with a word that causes them to be an incomplete thought.

> In this book you have learned three types of dependent clauses.
>> A *who/which* clause begins with *who* or *which*.
>> A *that* clause begins with *that*.
>> An adverb clause begins with a www word.
>
> A dependent clause must be added to a main clause.

Dependent Clause

Contains:
subject + verb

cannot stand alone

Main Clause
A **main clause** is a clause because it contains a subject and a verb. A main clause expresses a complete thought, so it can stand alone as a sentence.

[Families lived in the forest].
> Every sentence must have a main clause.

[Families lived in the forest] (because they lost their homes).
> In addition to a main clause, a sentence may include one or more dependent clauses.

MC Main Clause

Contains:
subject + verb

stands alone

Mark It!   Place square brackets around the main clause *[MC]*.
Write *v* above each verb and *s* above each subject.

                s   v
Usually, [Robin practiced archery in the morning].

When you mark the main clause with square brackets, begin with the subject of the main clause. Sometimes, an article or adjectives will come before the subject.

Think About It!
The word *because* usually begins an adverb clause. However, when *because* is followed by *of*, the two words together are a preposition.

> Adverb Clause: Robin aimed carefully (because he wanted the prize).
>
>> *Because he wanted the prize* is an adverb clause.
>> **PATTERN** www word (because) + subject (he) + verb (wanted)
>
> Prepositional Phrase: Robin aimed carefully because of the prize.
>
>> *Because of the prize* is a prepositional phrase.
>> **PATTERN** preposition (because of) + noun (prize) (no verb)

Read It!	**Mark It!**	**Fix It!**	Week 10
			Day 1

1 vocabulary

1 noun (n)
3 pronouns (pr)
1 adjective (adj)
1 *who/which* clause (w/w)
1 *that* clause (that)
1 [main clause]
3 subject-verb pairs (s v)
1 opener

1 capital
1 end mark

robin's followers **declared** that they would rob everyone who had robbed them

Rewrite It!

Week 10

Day 2

Read It!	Mark It!	Fix It!
1 vocabulary	1 article (ar)	2 capitals
	5 nouns (n)	1 comma
	1 pronoun (pr)	1 end mark
	3 adjectives (adj)	1 homophone
	1 adverb (adv)	
	2 coordinating conjunctions (cc)	
	1 adverb clause (AC)	
	1 [main clause]	
	2 subject-verb pairs (s v)	
	1 opener	

especially if powerful men **plundered** the poor,

robin and his men would recapture there goods,

and would return them

Rewrite It! _____

_____

_____

_____

_____

Week 10
Day 3

Read It!

1 vocabulary

Mark It!

4 nouns (n)
1 pronoun
1 adjective (adj)
1 coordinating conjunction (cc)
2 prepositional phrases
1 [main clause]
1 subject-verb pair (s v)
1 opener

Fix It!

1 capital
1 comma
1 end mark

to those in need, these men would offer **aid**,

and protection

Rewrite It!

Week 10

Day 4

Read It!

1 vocabulary

Mark It!

1 article (ar)
3 nouns (n)
2 pronouns (pr)
2 adverbs (adv)
1 coordinating conjunction (cc)
1 *that* clause (that)
1 [main clause]
2 subject-verb pairs (s v)
1 opener

Fix It!

1 capital
2 commas
1 end mark

they **earnestly** swore that they would never harm a maid wife or widow

Rewrite It! _____

_____

_____

_____

Learn It!

Who/Which Clause

A ***who/which* clause** is a dependent clause that begins with the word *who* or *which*.

A *who/which* clause can also begin with the word *whose*, the possessive case of *who* and *which*.

When *whose* begins a *who/which* clause, *whose* will not function as the subject of the clause because *whose* functions as a possessive adjective and shows ownership.

Robin, ~~Robin's~~ whose arrow broke, missed the mark.

The two sentences *Robin missed the mark* and *Robin's arrow broke* have been combined with a *who/which* clause. *Whose* takes the place of the possessive adjective *Robin's*.

Mark It!   Place parentheses around the *who/which* clause and write *w/w* above the word *who* or *which*. Write *v* above each verb and *s* above each subject.

```
         s        v     v
   w/w
The men (whose lands were taken) hid in the forest.
```

Dependent Clause

Who/Which Clause

Contains:
subject + verb

First Word:
who, which, whose

Commas:
unless essential

Marking:
w/w

Run-On

A **run-on** occurs when a sentence has main clauses that are not connected properly.

A **fused sentence** is two main clauses placed in one sentence without any punctuation between them. This is a common type of run-on error. The easiest way to fix this error is to place a period at the end of each main clause.

Find It!   Look for two main clauses that are missing a period between them.

Fix It!   Correct a fused sentence by putting a period between the main clauses. Capitalize the first word of the new sentence.

```
  s    v            v                s    v
[The men could not pay their taxes]. [they hid in
                                      ≡
the forest].
```

Fused sentence:
MC MC

This pattern is always wrong!

Fix:
MC. MC.

Think About It!

Many words can be used as different parts of speech. However, a word can perform only one part of speech at a time. For example, *swimming* can be a verb, adjective, or noun.

Verb: Robin was swimming in the river.

> In this sentence *swimming* is a verb because it follows the helping verb *was*. A word that ends in -ing functions as a verb only if it follows a helping verb.

Adjective: Robin jumped into the swimming hole.

> In this sentence *swimming* describes *hole*. What kind of hole? *swimming*. An adjective describes a noun or pronoun.

Noun: Swimming was Robin's favorite summer activity.

> In this sentence *swimming* is a thing. A noun is a person, place, thing, or idea.

Week 11
Day 1

Read It!

1 vocabulary

Mark It!

2 articles (ar)
6 nouns (n)
2 pronouns (pr)
4 adjectives (adj)
3 <u>prepositional phrases</u>
1 *who/which* clause (w/w)
2 [main clauses]
3 subject-verb pairs (s v)
2 openers

Fix It!

2 capitals
2 end marks

because of the desperate times, these men, whose families were hungry, stole money from **corrupt** noblemen they gave it to the peasants

Rewrite It!

Week 11
Day 2

Read It!
- 1 vocabulary

Mark It!
- 1 article (ar)
- 5 nouns (n)
- 1 pronoun (pr)
- 4 adjectives (adj)
- 1 adverb (adv)
- 1 coordinating conjunction
- 1 <u>prepositional phrase</u>
- 2 [main clauses]
- 2 subject-verb pairs (s v)
- 2 openers

Fix It!
- 3 capitals
- 1 comma
- 2 end marks
- 1 homophone

the peasants loved robin, and his merry men

they often told tales of there **courageous** deeds

Rewrite It! _____

Week 11
Day 3

Read It!

1 vocabulary

Mark It!

4 nouns (n)
1 pronoun (pr)
2 adjectives (adj)
2 adverbs (adv)
1 coordinating conjunction (cc)
1 prepositional phrase
1 adverb clause (AC)
1 [main clause]
2 subject-verb pairs (s v)
1 opener

Fix It!

2 capitals
1 end mark
1 homophone

repeatedly robin and his men moved there camp

because they were always in **peril**

Rewrite It!

Read It!	Mark It!	Fix It!	Week 11
1 vocabulary	2 articles (ar)	1 capital	Day 4
	6 nouns (n)	2 commas	
	3 adjectives (adj)	1 end mark	
	1 coordinating conjunction (cc)		
	2 <u>prepositional phrases</u>		
	1 [main clause]		
	1 subject-verb pair (s v)		
	1 opener		

for entertainment the men enjoyed competitions target practice and fishing in the cold, **gurgling** brook

Rewrite It! _____

Week 12

Learn It!

#5 Clausal Opener

A **#5 clausal opener** is a sentence that begins with an adverb clause.

The #5 clausal opener begins with a www word: when, while, where, as, since, if, although, because. It must contain a subject and a verb.

Pattern:
www word + subject + verb

(While the men relaxed)

This is an incorrect sentence fragment. A group of words is not a sentence unless it includes a main clause.

(While the men relaxed), [Robin was restless].

The #5 clausal opener will always have a comma and a main clause after it.

Mark It! Write ⑤ above the first word of a sentence that starts with an adverb clause.

⑤
AC   S   V
(Since Robin was restless), [he looked for adventure].

Comma

A **comma** is used to separate items in a sentence. Week 8 you learned that a comma is used after but not before an adverb clause.

Fix It! Add a comma after an adverb clause.
Remove a comma before an adverb clause.

AC
(While his men rested), [Robin set out].

                    AC
[Robin left his men], (because he wanted adventure).

, AC, MC

✗ MC AC

Week 12
Day 1

Read It! **Mark It!** **Fix It!**

1 vocabulary

3 articles (ar)
3 nouns (n)
1 pronoun (pr)
1 adjective (adj)
1 adverb (adv)
1 coordinating conjunction (cc)
2 prepositional phrases
2 [main clauses]
2 subject-verb pairs (s v)
2 openers

2 capitals
1 comma
2 end marks

the children of the merry men **romped** along the bank

they laughed, and joked together

Rewrite It!

Week 12
Day 2

Read It!
1 vocabulary

Mark It!
4 nouns (n)
3 pronouns (pr)
5 adjectives (adj)
1 adverb (adv)
1 prepositional phrase
1 adverb clause (AC)
3 [main clauses]
4 subject-verb pairs (s v)
1 opener

Fix It!
3 capitals
2 commas
1 end mark
1 apostrophe
1 number

although everyone seemed happy robin was **restless**. "for 14 days weve enjoyed very little sport my friends," he complained

Rewrite It! _____
_____
_____
_____

Week 12
Day 3

Read It!
1 vocabulary

Mark It!
3 nouns (n)
3 pronouns (pr)
1 adverb (adv)
2 prepositional phrases
1 adverb clause (AC)
2 [main clauses]
3 subject-verb pairs (s v)

Fix It!
4 capitals
1 comma
1 end mark
1 homophone

"while i journey to nottingham too seek adventures you can wait for me here," robin **directed**

Rewrite It!

Week 12
Day 4

Read It!

1 vocabulary

Mark It!

4 nouns (n)
3 pronouns (pr)
5 adjectives (adj)
1 adverb (adv)
1 prepositional phrase
1 *who/which* clause (w/w)
1 *that* clause (that)
1 adverb clause (AC)
1 [main clause]
4 subject-verb pairs (s v)
1 opener

Fix It!

1 capital
1 comma
1 end mark
1 number

he told his men that they should come quickly, when they heard his **signal**, which would be 3 short blasts on his bugle

Rewrite It!

Learn It!

#6 Vss Opener

A **#6 vss opener** is a very short sentence.

Very short means two to five words. *Sentence* means it must have a main clause.

Robin sought adventure.

This sentence is short because it has three words.
It is a sentence because it has a main clause. It is a #6 vss opener.

Mark It!   Write ⑥ above the first word of a very short sentence.

⑥
      S   V
[The wet log wobbled].

Run-On

A **run-on** occurs when a sentence has main clauses that are not connected properly.

Week 11 you learned that a **fused sentence** is two main clauses placed in one sentence without any punctuation between them. This is one type of run-on error.

A **comma splice** is two main clauses placed in one sentence with only a comma between them. This is a second type of run-on error. The easiest way to fix both of these errors is to place a period at the end of each main clause.

Find It!   Look for two main clauses that have only a comma between them.

Fix It!   Correct a comma splice by replacing the comma with a period. Capitalize the first word of the new sentence.

S   V   S   V
[Robin noticed a log across a stream], [the log looked sturdy].

Fused sentence:
MC MC

Comma Splice:
MC, MC

These patterns are always wrong!

Fix:
MC. MC.

Impostor -ly Adverb

An **impostor -ly adverb** is a word that looks like an adverb because it ends in -ly but is actually an adjective. Although many adverbs end in -ly, some adjectives also end in -ly. If the -ly word describes a noun or pronoun, it is an impostor -ly adverb. Only adjectives describe nouns.

Mark It!   Write *adv* above each adverb. Write *adj* above each adjective.

     adj   *adv*   *adj*
The sturdy log safely spanned the chilly stream.

			Week 13
Read It!	**Mark It!**	**Fix It!**	Day 1
1 vocabulary	1 article (ar)	3 capitals	
	3 nouns (n)	1 comma	
	1 pronoun (pr)	2 end marks	
	2 prepositional phrases		
	2 [main clauses]		
	2 subject-verb pairs (s v)		
	2 openers		

robin hood **roamed** through the forest, he searched for adventure

Rewrite It! _____

Week 13 — Day 2

Read It!	Mark It!	Fix It!
1 vocabulary	5 articles (ar)	2 capitals
	6 nouns (n)	1 comma
	4 adjectives (adj)	1 end mark
	1 coordinating conjunction (cc)	
	3 <u>prepositional phrases</u>	
	1 *who/which* clause (w/w)	
	1 [main clause]	
	2 subject-verb pairs (s v)	
	1 opener	

at a sharp curve in a path, robin neared a log,

which **spanned** a broad pebbly stream, and acted

as a narrow bridge

Rewrite It! _____

Read It!	Mark It!	Fix It!	Week 13
			Day 3
1 vocabulary	4 articles (ar)	1 capital	
	4 nouns (n)	1 comma	
	2 pronouns (pr)	1 end mark	
	3 adjectives (adj)		
	1 prepositional phrase		
	1 *who/which* clause (w/w)		
	1 adverb clause (AC)		
	1 [main clause]		
	3 subject-verb pairs (s v)		
	1 opener		

as he approached the log he noticed a large, **stout** stranger, who was approaching the log from the other side

Rewrite It! _____

Week 13

Day 4

Read It!	Mark It!	Fix It!
1 vocabulary	1 article (ar)	3 capitals
	3 nouns (n)	1 comma
	1 pronoun (pr)	3 end marks
	1 adjective (adj)	1 homophone
	1 adverb	
	3 [main clauses]	
	3 subject-verb pairs (s v)	
	3 openers	

robin **quickened** his pace the stranger did

to, both wanted to cross

Rewrite It! _____

Learn It!

Interjection

An **interjection** expresses an emotion.

> Wow! He hit the bull's-eye!
>
> When an interjection expresses a strong emotion, use an exclamation mark.
> Capitalize the word that follows an exclamation mark.

> Hmm, he still has one arrow.
>
> When an interjection does not express a strong emotion, use a comma.
> Do not capitalize the word that follows a comma.

Capitalization

Capitalize an interjection when it is the first word of a sentence.

Capitalize a word that follows an exclamation mark.

Mark It!   Write *int* above each interjection.

Fix It!   Place a comma or an exclamation mark after each interjection.
Place three short lines below letters that should be capitalized.

   int
Yikes! he killed the king's deer!

Imperative Sentence (Implied Subject)

An **imperative sentence** gives a command or makes a request.

Every verb has a subject, a noun or pronoun that performs the verb action. However, the imperative sentence does not have a written subject. Rather, the subject is implied.

Because commands are always directed toward someone or something, the subject of an imperative sentence is always *you*.

Find It!   Read the sentence and look for the verb. Ask, "Who or what ___ (verb)?"
If the sentence forms a command, the subject is *you*.

Mark It!   Write (you) in parentheses to show the subject.
Write *v* above each verb and *s* above *you*.

  s   *v*
(you) Step up to the mark.

---

8 Parts of Speech

Interjection
Definition:

An interjection expresses an emotion.

Homophone

A **homophone** is a word that sounds like another word but is spelled differently and has a different meaning. Correctly use the homophones *whose* and *who's*.

Whose is a possessive pronoun: *whose* arrows (the arrows belong to whom).

The relative pronoun *whose* functions as a possessive adjective and begins a *who/which* clause.

Who's is a contraction: *who's* tired (who is tired).

The contraction *who's* is a shortened form of *who is* and functions as the subject pronoun (who) and verb (is) of the clause

Fix It! Place a line through the incorrect homophone and write the correct word above it.

Whose ~~Who's~~ bow is this? ~~Whose~~ *Who's* ready to shoot next?

Week 14
Day 1

Read It!	**Mark It!**	**Fix It!**
1 vocabulary	2 articles (ar)	3 capitals
	3 nouns (n)	1 comma
	1 pronoun (pr)	1 end mark
	1 adjective (adj)	1 homophone
	3 adverbs (adv)
	1 *who/which* clause (w/w)
	3 [main clauses]
	4 subject-verb pairs (s v)

"go back sir," demanded robin **rudely**.

"the one whose the better man should cross first"

Rewrite It! _____

Week 14
Day 2

Read It!	**Mark It!**	**Fix It!**

1 vocabulary

2 articles (ar)
2 nouns (n)
2 pronouns (pr)
2 adjectives (adj)
1 adverb (adv)
3 [main clauses]
3 subject-verb pairs (s v)
1 opener

3 capitals
2 end marks

the **confident** stranger responded, "you go back i am the better man"

Rewrite It! _____

Week 14
Day 3

Read It!
1 vocabulary

Mark It!
2 nouns (n)
3 pronouns (pr)
2 adjectives (adj)
3 adverbs (adv)
1 coordinating conjunction (cc)
1 adverb clause (AC)
1 [main clause]
2 subject-verb pairs (s v)
1 opener

Fix It!
2 capitals
2 commas
1 end mark

naturally, this **riled** robin, since his merry men always respected him, and obeyed him immediately

Rewrite It! _____

Week 14
Day 4

Read It!	Mark It!	Fix It!
1 vocabulary	2 articles (ar)	6 capitals
	2 nouns (n)	1 comma
	6 pronouns (pr)	5 end marks
	1 adjective (adj)	3 apostrophes
	2 adverbs (adv)	
	1 interjection (int)	
	1 <u>prepositional phrase</u>	
	1 *that* clause (that)	
	1 adverb clause (AC)	
	4 [main clauses]	
	6 subject-verb pairs (s v)	

"if you dont go back ill fire an arrow at you"

asserted robin

"hah do you think that im afraid" the

other mocked

Rewrite It! _____

Week 15

Learn It!

Quotation Marks—Capitalization and End Marks

Quotation marks indicate words are spoken. The quote is the sentence in quotation marks. The attribution is the person speaking and the speaking verb.

The stranger cried, "Obviously, I am not afraid."
    The attribution may come before the quoted sentence.
    Attribution, "Quote."

"Obviously, I am not afraid," the stranger cried.
    The attribution may come after the quoted sentence.
    "Quote," attribution.

"Obviously," the stranger cried, "I am not afraid."
    The attribution may come in the middle of the quoted sentence.
    "Quote," attribution, "rest of quoted sentence."

"You can cross the stream after I do."
    Sometimes a quoted sentence will not have an attribution.

Regardless of where the attribution comes in relation to the quoted sentence, capitalization and punctuation rules remain the same.

    Place quotation marks around the words that are spoken.

    Capitalize the first word of the quoted sentence.

    Capitalize the first word of the attribution when it begins the sentence.

    If the quoted sentence makes a statement, place a period inside the closing quotation mark unless the attribution follows.
        Attribution, "Quote."
        "Quote," attribution.

    If the quoted sentence asks a question, place a question mark inside the closing quotation mark.
        Attribution, "Quote?"
        "Quote?" attribution.

    If the quoted sentence expresses strong emotion, place an exclamation mark inside the closing quotation mark.
        Attribution, "Quote!"
        "Quote!" attribution.

Comma

A **comma** is used to separate items in a sentence.

    Use a comma to separate an attribution from a direct quote.

Fix It!   Place quotation marks around the words that are spoken.
          Place three short lines below letters that should be capitalized.
          Place the correct end mark at the end of each sentence.
          Place a comma between an attribution and a quote.

robin demanded, "get off the log."

"you don't scare me," the stranger replied.

Indentation

An **indentation** is a blank space between the margin and the beginning of a line of text. It shows the start of a new paragraph.

In fiction (stories), there are four reasons to start a new paragraph.

New Speaker: Start a new paragraph when a new character speaks. Include the attribution with the quotation. Sentences before or after the quotation that point directly to the quotation can remain in the same paragraph.

New Topic: Start a new paragraph when the narrator or a character switches the topic.

New Place: Start a new paragraph when the story switches to a new location. If several switches are made in quick succession, such as a character's journey to find something, it may be less choppy to keep in one paragraph.

New Time: Start a new paragraph when the time changes.

Fix It!   Add the ¶ symbol or an arrow ➔ in front of each sentence that should start a new paragraph.

Robin approached the log.

¶ "Stand back!" cried the stranger.

When you rewrite the passage, indent. Start the sentence on the next line and write ½ inch from the left margin.

Week 15

Day 1

Read It!   **Mark It!**   **Fix It!**

1 vocabulary   1 article (ar)   1 indent
                   4 nouns (n)   3 capitals
                   2 pronouns (pr)   4 quotation marks
                   2 adjectives (adj)   2 end marks
                   2 <u>prepositional phrases</u>   1 homophone
                   3 [main clauses]
                   3 subject-verb pairs (s v)

you joke like a fool **bellowed** robin. i could

fire this arrow through you're heart

Rewrite It! _____

_____

_____

_____

Week 15
Day 2

Read It!	Mark It!	Fix It!
1 vocabulary	4 articles (ar)	1 indent
	4 nouns (n)	4 capitals
	3 pronouns (pr)	2 commas
	2 adjectives (adj)	2 quotation marks
	2 adverbs (adv)	3 end marks
	1 <u>prepositional phrase</u>	
	4 [main clauses]	
	4 subject-verb pairs (s v)	
	1 opener	

the tall stranger chuckled you stand there with a **lethal** bow i only carry a staff, are you a coward

Rewrite It! _____

Week 15 — Day 3

Read It! **Mark It!** **Fix It!**

1 vocabulary

2 articles (ar)
4 nouns (n)
4 pronouns (pr)
1 adjective (adj)
2 adverbs (adv)
1 *who/which* clause (w/w)
1 *that* clause (that)
3 [main clauses]
5 subject-verb pairs (s v)

1 indent
3 capitals
3 quotation marks
2 end marks
1 homophone
2 apostrophes

i have never been called a coward cried robin,

who's face became **crimson**. ill teach you a lesson

that you wont forget

No closing quotation mark because quote continues.

Rewrite It! _____

Week 15

Day 4

Read It!	Mark It!	Fix It!
1 vocabulary	1 article (ar)	4 capitals
	2 nouns (n)	1 comma
	3 pronouns (pr)	1 quotation mark
	2 adjectives (adj)	1 end mark
	2 adverb clauses (AC)	1 homophone
	2 [main clauses]	
	4 subject-verb pairs (s v)	

No opening quotation mark because quote continues.

stay where you are! after i make a staff

i will test you're **sparring** skills

Rewrite It! _____

Learn It!

Coordinating Conjunction

A **coordinating conjunction** connects the same type of words, phrases, or clauses. Week 2 you learned two comma rules to use when a sentence has a coordinating conjunction (for, and, nor, but, or, yet, so).

FANBOYS

> Robin was kind, funny, and brave.

In this sentence the coordinating conjunction *and* connects three adjectives: *kind*, *funny*, and *brave*. Two comma are used.

a, b, and c

> Robin was kind and funny.

In this sentence the coordinating conjunction *and* connects two adjectives: *kind* and *funny*. No comma is used.

a and b

Today you will learn two more comma rules. Compare these sentences:

> The stranger waited and whistled a tune.

In this sentence the coordinating conjunction *and* connects two verbs: *waited* and *whistled*. No comma is used. This is the same pattern as **a and b** when *a* and *b* are verbs.

MC cc 2nd verb

> The stranger waited, and Robin whistled a tune.

In this sentence the coordinating conjunction *and* connects two main clauses: *stranger waited*, and *Robin whistled*. One comma is used.

MC, cc MC

Comma

A **comma** is used to separate items in a sentence.

✗ Do not use a comma before a coordinating conjunction when it connects two verbs.
PATTERN MC cc 2nd verb

; Use a comma before a coordinating conjunction when it connects two main clauses.
PATTERN MC, cc MC

Mark It! Write *cc* above each coordinating conjunction.

Fix It! Remove a comma before a *cc* that connects two verbs.
Add a comma before a *cc* that connects two main clauses.

```
    S        V          cc      V
[Robin agreed to spar, and made a staff].
    S        V       ⌐ cc   S     V
[Robin agreed to spar], and [he made a staff].
```

MC cc 2nd verb or MC, cc MC

Read each sentence and decide if the coordinating conjunction connects verbs or clauses.
  If the coordinating conjunction connects main clauses, insert a comma.
  Circle the correct comma rule pattern.

Robin accepted the challenge and collected his arrows.

   MC cc 2nd verb   **MC, cc MC**

Robin accepted the challenge and he collected his arrows.

   MC cc 2nd verb   **MC, cc MC**

The waterfall spilled over the cliff and it created a whirlpool.

   MC cc 2nd verb   **MC, cc MC**

The waterfall spilled over the cliff and created a whirlpool.

   MC cc 2nd verb   **MC, cc MC**

Little John released the arrow but surprisingly missed the target.

   MC cc 2nd verb   **MC, cc MC**

Little John released the arrow but he missed the target.

   MC cc 2nd verb   **MC, cc MC**

Robin was an outlaw so he could not return home.

   MC cc 2nd verb   **MC, cc MC**

Robin was an outlaw and could not return home.

   MC cc 2nd verb   **MC, cc MC**

Read It!   **Mark It!**   **Fix It!**   Week 16 / Day 1

1 vocabulary

- 2 articles (ar)
- 3 nouns (n)
- 3 pronouns (pr)
- 2 adjectives (adj)
- 2 prepositional phrases
- 3 [main clauses]
- 3 subject-verb pairs (s v)

- 1 indent
- 2 capitals
- 1 comma
- 4 quotation marks
- 1 end mark
- 1 homophone
- 1 apostrophe

i welcome you to try **countered** the stranger with a twinkle in his eye. im happy too wait

Rewrite It!

Week 16

Day 2

Read It!	Mark It!	Fix It!
1 vocabulary	1 article (ar)	3 capitals
	3 nouns (n)	2 commas
	2 pronouns (pr)	1 end mark
	2 adjectives (adj)	1 homophone
	3 adverbs (adv)	
	1 coordinating conjunction (cc)	
	2 <u>prepositional phrases</u>	
	1 adverb clause (AC)	
	2 [main clauses]	
	3 subject-verb pairs (s v)	
	2 openers	

patiently the calm giant leaned on his staff, and waited

their for robin. he whistled, as he **gazed** about

Rewrite It! _____

Week 16
Day 3

Read It!

1 vocabulary

Mark It!

3 articles (ar)
6 nouns (n)
3 adjectives (adj)
1 coordinating conjunction (cc)
2 prepositional phrases
1 who/which clause (w/w)
1 [main clause]
2 subject-verb pairs (s v)
1 opener

Fix It!

1 indent
2 capitals
2 commas
1 end mark
1 number

robin hood stepped into the forest found a tall oak and cut a **sturdy** staff, which measured 6 feet in length

Rewrite It! _____

_____

_____

_____

Week 16
Day 4

Read It!	Mark It!	Fix It!
1 vocabulary	1 article (ar)	2 capitals
	4 nouns (n)	1 comma
	2 pronouns (pr)	2 end marks
	3 adjectives (adj)	1 number
	2 adverbs (adv)	
	1 coordinating conjunction (cc)	
	3 [main clauses]	
	3 subject-verb pairs (s v)	
	2 openers	

robin **fashioned** his weapon he secretly studied

the giant and he confidently planned his 1st move

Rewrite It!

Week 17

Learn It!

Phrase versus Clause

A **phrase** is a group of related words that contains either a noun or a verb, never both.
   The most common phrase is the prepositional phrase, which never has a verb.
A **clause** is a group of related words that contains both a subject and a verb.
   A **main clause** stands alone as a sentence. It expresses a complete thought.
   A **dependent clause** cannot stand alone as a sentence. It must be added to a sentence that is already complete.
      You have learned three types of dependent clauses: *who/which* clauses, *that* clauses, and adverb clauses.

Decide if the following is a phrase or a clause. Circle the correct answer.

he approached the log	phrase	clause
near the tall oak tree	phrase	clause
that was a hundred years old	phrase	clause
where a stranger stood	phrase	clause
beneath a full moon	phrase	clause
which shone brightly	phrase	clause

Dependent clauses begin with a word that causes them to be an incomplete thought. Draw lines to connect the type of clause to the word that would begin the clause.

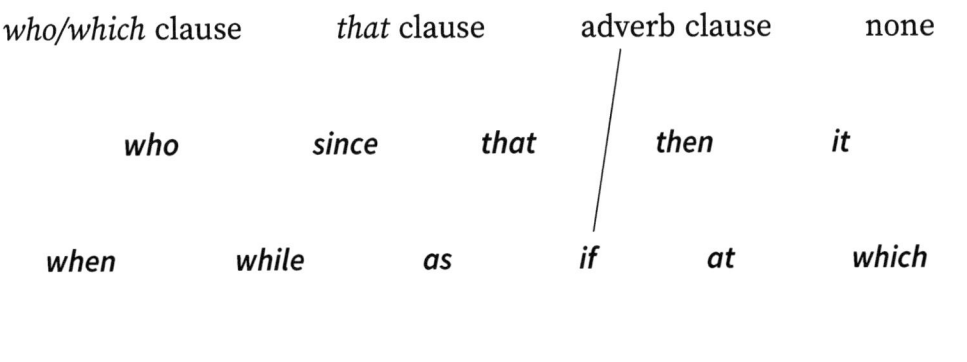

who/which clause   *that* clause   adverb clause   none

who   since   that   then   it

when   while   as   if   at   which

Every clause contains a _____ and a _____ .

Institute for Excellence in Writing *Fix It! Grammar: Robin Hood* Student Book Level 3   97

Week 17

Day 1

Read It!

1 vocabulary

Mark It!

1 article (ar)
4 nouns (n)
1 pronoun (pr)
2 adjectives (adj)
2 adverbs (adv)
2 <u>prepositional phrases</u>
2 [main clauses]
2 subject-verb pairs (s v)
2 openers

Fix It!

4 capitals
2 end marks

until that day robin had never met a larger man

usually, robin **towered** over others

Rewrite It! _____

Week 17

Day 2

Read It!	Mark It!	Fix It!
1 vocabulary	3 articles (ar)	3 capitals
	6 nouns (n)	1 comma
	6 adjectives (adj)	1 end mark
	1 adverb clause (AC)	2 numbers
	2 [main clauses]	
	3 subject-verb pairs (s v)	
	2 openers	

this **rival** was a 7-foot man! although robin's shoulders were broad the stranger's shoulders were 2 times the size

Rewrite It!

Read It!	Mark It!	Fix It!	
			Week 17
			Day 3
1 vocabulary	2 nouns (n)	3 capitals	
	2 pronouns (pr)	2 commas	
	5 adjectives (adj)	1 end mark	
	1 adverb (adv)		
	1 coordinating conjunction (cc)		
	1 who/which clause (w/w)		
	1 that clause (that)		
	2 [main clauses]		
	4 subject-verb pairs (s v)		
	2 openers		

carefully robin **crafted** his weapon, which must be strong straight and sturdy. he was determined that he would win

Rewrite It!

Week 17
Day 4

Read It!	**Mark It!**	**Fix It!**

Read It!
1 vocabulary

Mark It!
1 article (ar)
5 nouns (n)
2 pronouns (pr)
2 adjectives (adj)
1 coordinating conjunction (cc)
1 prepositional phrase
1 adverb clause (AC)
3 [main clauses]
4 subject-verb pairs (s v)
2 openers

Fix It!
4 capitals
2 commas
1 end mark
1 homophone

as robin worked he smiled for he had found his adventure. despite it's **risk** robin welcomed a challenge

Rewrite It!

Learn It!

Usage

Some words are close in spelling but have different meanings and uses. Correctly use the words *then* and *than*.

Then is an adverb meaning next or immediately after.

Then Robin approached the log. It was then Robin's turn.

Than is a word used to show a comparison.

The stranger was taller than Robin.

Fix It!   Place a line through the incorrect word and write the correct word above it.

Then   **than**
~~Than~~ Robin, who was smaller ~~then~~ the stranger, taunted him.

Week 18
Day 1

Read It!

1 vocabulary

Mark It!

1 article (ar)
3 nouns (n)
3 pronouns (pr)
2 adjectives (adj)
1 adverb (adv)
1 adverb clause (AC)
3 [main clauses]
4 subject-verb pairs (s v)
1 opener

Fix It!

1 indent
4 capitals
2 commas
1 quotation
1 end mark
1 apostrophe

robin hood then **goaded** the giant man. im ready stranger. fight me, if you dare

No closing quotation mark because quote continues.

Rewrite It! _____

Week 18

Read It!	Mark It!	Fix It!	Day 2
1 vocabulary	3 articles (ar)	1 capital	
	3 nouns (n)	1 comma	
	2 pronouns (pr)	1 quotation	
	1 adjective (adj)	1 end mark	
	1 adverb (adv)	1 usage	
	2 <u>prepositional phrases</u>		
	1 adverb clause (AC)		
	1 [main clause]		
	2 subject-verb pairs (s v)		

No opening quotation mark because quote continues.

when one of us falls into the stream than the

victor will be the better man

Rewrite It! _____

_____

_____

_____

Week 18 — Day 3

Read It!
- 1 vocabulary

Mark It!
- 4 articles (ar)
- 4 nouns (n)
- 2 pronouns (pr)
- 3 adjectives (adj)
- 3 adverbs (adv)
- 1 interjection
- 1 prepositional phrase
- 1 *who/which* clause (w/w)
- 3 [main clauses]
- 4 subject-verb pairs (s v)

Fix It!
- 1 indent
- 2 capitals
- 2 commas
- 4 quotations
- 1 end mark
- 1 apostrophe

ah its a fair test agreed the stranger. he who is more **adept** with the staff is most certainly the better man

Rewrite It!

Week 18

Day 4

Read It!	Mark It!	Fix It!
1 vocabulary	3 articles (ar)	1 indent
	6 nouns (n)	3 capitals
	1 pronoun (pr)	2 commas
	2 adjectives (adj)	2 end marks
	1 adverb (adv)	
	3 <u>prepositional phrases</u>	
	1 adverb clause (AC)	
	2 [main clauses]	
	3 subject-verb pairs (s v)	
	2 openers	

the giant **nimbly** twirled his staff above his head, it whistled through the air, as robin stepped onto the log

Rewrite It! _____

_____

_____

_____

_____

Learn It!

Possessive Adjective

An **adjective** describes a noun or pronoun.

> An adjective tells which one, what kind, how many, or whose.
>
> When a noun is followed by an apostrophe + s, it functions as a possessive adjective and shows ownership. It answers the question *whose*.

Robin marveled at the stranger's skill.

> The noun *stranger* is followed by an apostrophe + s. Because *stranger's* functions as a possessive adjective, we call it an adjective, not a noun.
> Whose skill? *stranger's*
>
> Without the apostrophe, the noun would be plural.
> There are not several *strangers* (plural).

Find It! Look for nouns that show ownership or possession. They will end in *s* and answer the question *whose*.

Fix It! Place an apostrophe before the *s* to show that the noun is functioning as a possessive adjective.

Mark It! Write *adj* above each adjective.

                                  adj
The stranger dodged Robin's blow.

Think About It!

> Many words can be used as different parts of speech. However, a word can perform only one part of speech at a time.
>
> Plural Noun: The foresters mocked Robin.
>
>> In this sentence *foresters* ends with an *s*. The *s* indicates that *foresters* is a plural noun. There is more than one forester.
>
> Possessive Adjective: The forester's mockery angered Robin.
>
>> In this sentence *forester's* ends with an apostrophe + s. The apostrophe + s indicates that *forester's* is a possessive adjective. Whose mockery? *forester's*

Week 19
Day 1

Read It!

1 vocabulary

Mark It!

4 articles (ar)
6 nouns (n)
1 pronoun (pr)
3 adjectives (adj)
2 adverbs (adv)
1 coordinating conjunction (cc)
2 prepositional phrases
2 [main clauses]
2 subject-verb pairs (s v)
2 openers

Fix It!

3 capitals
1 comma
2 end marks
1 usage
1 apostrophe

quickly robin approached his **adversary** on the bridge he dodged the stranger's staff, and than returned a blow to the strangers head

Rewrite It! _____

Week 19
Day 2

Read It!	Mark It!	Fix It!
1 vocabulary	3 articles (ar)	3 capitals
	5 nouns (n)	1 comma
	1 pronoun (pr)	1 end mark
	2 adjectives (adj)	1 apostrophe
	1 coordinating conjunction (cc)	
	2 <u>prepositional phrases</u>	
	3 [main clauses]	
	3 subject-verb pairs (s v)	
	2 openers	

most would have tumbled into the water but the stranger **parried** robins blow to the right. both men began to sweat

Rewrite It! _____

Read It!   **Mark It!**   **Fix It!**   Week 19 / Day 3

Read It!	Mark It!	Fix It!
1 vocabulary	2 articles (ar)	2 capitals
	4 nouns (n)	1 end mark
	1 pronoun (pr)	1 number
	3 adjectives (adj)	
	2 adverbs (adv)	
	1 <u>prepositional phrase</u>	
	2 [main clauses]	
	2 subject-verb pairs (s v)	
	2 openers	

in response the 7-foot man fiercely returned another blow. it would have easily **leveled** a weaker opponent

Rewrite It! _____

Week 19

Day 4

Read It!	Mark It!	Fix It!
1 vocabulary	2 articles (ar)	3 capitals
	4 nouns (n)	1 comma
	3 pronouns (pr)	1 end mark
	2 adjectives (adj)	1 apostrophe
	2 adverbs (adv)	
	1 <u>prepositional phrase</u>	
	1 *that* clause (that)	
	1 adverb clause (AC)	
	1 [main clause]	
	3 subject-verb pairs (s v)	
	1 opener	

when robin hood **deftly** pushed the opponents staff to the side he showed him that this was no easy fight

Rewrite It! _____

Learn It!

Adverb Clause

An **adverb clause** is a group of words that begins with a www word and contains a subject and a verb. An adverb clause is a dependent clause, which means it must be added to a sentence that is already complete.

Week 8 you learned that an adverb clause begins with a www word. A www word is called a subordinating conjunction. The acronym *www.asia.b* reminds us of the eight most common subordinating conjunctions.

Memorize It! **when   while   where   as   since   if   although   because**

These are not the only words that begin an adverb clause. Other words can function as www words too.

Memorize It! **after   before   until   unless   whenever   whereas   than**

A www word must have a subject and verb after it to begin an adverb clause.

Mark It! Place parentheses around the adverb clause and write *AC* above the www word. Write *v* above each verb and *s* above each subject.

                              AC   s   v

The stranger would cross (unless Robin stopped him).

Dependent Clause

Adverb Clause
Pattern:
www word + subject + verb

First Word:
www word

Commas:
after, not before

Marking:
AC

Adverb Clause or Prepositional Phrase

These words usually begin adverb clauses.

| when | while | where | **as** | since | if | although | **because** |
| **after** | **before** | **until** | unless | whenever | whereas | than | |

These words usually begin prepositional phrases.

aboard	around	between	in	opposite	toward
about	**as**	beyond	inside	out	under
above	at	by	instead of	outside	underneath
according to	**because of**	concerning	into	over	unlike
across	**before**	despite	like	past	**until**
after	behind	down	minus	regarding	unto
against	below	during	near	**since**	up, upon
along	beneath	except	of	through	with
amid	beside	for	off	throughout	within
among	besides	from	on, onto	to	without

Pattern:
www word + subject + verb

Pattern:
preposition + noun (no verb)

The words *after, as, because, before, since* and *until* appear on both lists. When you mark the sentences, consider the patterns.

    Adverb Clause: (Before they met), Robin won every fight.

        Before they met is an adverb clause.
        PATTERN www word (Before) + subject (they) + verb (met)

    Prepositional Phrase: <u>Before the fight</u> Robin was undefeated.

        Before the fight is a prepositional phrase.
        PATTERN preposition (Before) + noun (fight) (no verb)

Week 20

Read It! | **Mark It!** | **Fix It!** | Day 1

1 vocabulary

2 articles (ar)
2 nouns (n)
3 pronouns (pr)
1 prepositional phrase
1 adverb clause (AC)
2 [main clauses]
3 subject-verb pairs (s v)
2 openers

1 indent
1 comma
2 capitals
2 end marks

after an hour neither had **budged** an inch, both

stood where they had begun

Rewrite It! _____

Week 20

Day 2

Read It!	Mark It!	Fix It!
1 vocabulary	6 nouns (n)	2 capitals
	2 pronouns (pr)	2 commas
	4 adjectives (adj)	1 end mark
	1 adverb (adv)	2 homophones
	2 coordinating conjunctions (cc)	
	2 adverb clauses (AC)	
	2 [main clauses]	
	4 subject-verb pairs (s v)	
	2 openers	

as they **battled** both men gave, and received many blows until cuts and bruises covered there bodies. each had aching muscles to

Rewrite It! _____

			Week 20
Read It!	**Mark It!**	**Fix It!**	Day 3

Read It!: 1 vocabulary

Mark It!:
- 1 article (ar)
- 3 nouns (n)
- 1 pronoun (pr)
- 1 adverb (adv)
- 1 coordinating conjunction (cc)
- 2 <u>prepositional phrases</u>
- 1 [main clause]
- 1 subject-verb pair (s v)
- 1 opener

Fix It!:
- 1 capital
- 1 comma
- 1 end mark

despite **fatigue** neither considered quitting, or seemed likely to tumble off the bridge

Rewrite It!

Read It!	**Mark It!**	**Fix It!**	Week 20
			Day 4

1 vocabulary

2 articles (ar)
3 nouns (n)
1 pronoun (pr)
3 adjectives (adj)
3 adverbs (adv)
1 *that* clause (that)
1 adverb clause (AC)
1 [main clause]
3 subject-verb pairs (s v)
1 opener

1 capital
1 comma
1 end mark
1 number

as the 2 men rested each man **privately** believed that he had never met a more skillful opponent

Rewrite It! _____

Review It!

Week 21

Coordinating Conjunction
A **coordinating conjunction** connects the same type of words, phrases, or clauses.

Read each sentence and decide what the coordinating conjunction connects.
 If the coordinating conjunction connects main clauses, insert a comma.
 If the coordinating conjunction connects three items in a series, insert commas.
 Circle the correct comma rule pattern.

Robin lost the fight for he was thinking about a lovely maiden.

   MC, cc MC   MC cc 2nd verb   a and b   a, b, and c

Maid Marian was a noblewoman and lived in a castle.

   MC, cc MC   MC cc 2nd verb   a and b   a, b, and c

She had bright eyes and a warm smile.

   MC, cc MC   MC cc 2nd verb   a and b   a, b, and c

She could ride skillfully climb trees and shoot an arrow straight.

   MC, cc MC   MC cc 2nd verb   a and b   a, b, and c

Maid Marian was courageous and loyal to the men of Sherwood Forest.

   MC, cc MC   MC cc 2nd verb   a and b   a, b, and c

Maid Marian hated thievery but she pitied the poor.

   MC, cc MC   MC cc 2nd verb   a and b   a, b, and c

She was known for her beauty bravery and boldness.

   MC, cc MC   MC cc 2nd verb   a and b   a, b, and c

Later she married Robin Hood and joined him in Sherwood Forest.

   MC, cc MC   MC cc 2nd verb   a and b   a, b, and c

Read It!	Mark It!	Fix It!	Week 21
			Day 1
1 vocabulary	2 articles (ar)	1 indent	
	4 nouns (n)	3 capitals	
	1 pronoun (pr)	1 comma	
	3 adjectives (adj)	2 end marks	
	1 adverb (adv)	1 apostrophe	
	1 *who/which* clause (w/w)		
	1 adverb clause (AC)		
	2 [main clauses]		
	4 subject-verb pairs (s v)		
	2 openers		

although both were wounded the battle continued

finally, robin **delivered** a mighty blow, which struck

his opponents ribs

Rewrite It! _____

Week 21

Day 2

Read It!	Mark It!	Fix It!
1 vocabulary	1 article (ar)	3 capitals
	5 nouns (n)	2 commas
	1 pronoun (pr)	1 end mark
	3 adjectives (adj)	1 apostrophe
	2 adverbs (adv)	
	1 coordinating conjunction (cc)	
	1 <u>prepositional phrase</u>	
	2 [main clauses]	
	2 subject-verb pairs (s v)	
	2 openers	

instantly the stranger **recovered** raised his arms and brought his staff down on robins head. this caused blood to flow

Rewrite It! _____

Week 21

Read It! | **Mark It!** | **Fix It!** | Day 3

1 vocabulary

3 articles (ar)
5 nouns (n)
1 pronoun (pr)
2 adjectives (adj)
2 coordinating conjunctions (cc)
1 prepositional phrase
3 [main clauses]
3 subject-verb pairs (s v)
2 openers

4 capitals
1 comma
1 end mark
1 apostrophe

the jolt **inflamed** robin so he swung at the other man. the stranger ducked and avoided robins staff

Rewrite It! _____

Week 21

Day 4

Read It!

1 vocabulary

Mark It!

2 articles (ar)
5 nouns (n)
1 pronoun (pr)
2 adjectives (adj)
2 prepositional phrases
1 adverb clause (AC)
2 [main clauses]
3 subject-verb pairs (s v)
2 openers

Fix It!

3 capitals
1 comma
1 end mark

at once the stranger **counterattacked.** as robin lost his footing he tumbled into the chilly water

Rewrite It! _____

Learn It!

Pronoun

A **pronoun** replaces a noun in order to avoid repetition. It refers back to some person or thing recently mentioned and takes the place of that person or thing.

There are many types of pronouns. Week 1 you reviewed **personal pronouns,** which take the place of common and proper nouns. Week 9 you learned **indefinite pronouns,** which do not refer to any particular person or thing. Week 9 you also learned **demonstrative pronouns,** which point to a particular person or thing.

Review the pronoun lists in Appendix III.

A **reflexive pronoun** ends in -*self* (singular) or -*selves* (plural) and refers to the subject of the same sentence.

Mark It!   Write *pr* above each pronoun.

                  pr
The men hid themselves in the forest.

               pr
Robin stood up for himself.

Week 22

Read It!   **Mark It!**   **Fix It!**   Day 1

Read It!	Mark It!	Fix It!
1 vocabulary	1 noun (n)	2 capitals
	4 pronouns (pr)	2 commas
	2 adjectives (adj)	2 end marks
	1 adverb (adv)	
	1 <u>prepositional phrase</u>	
	1 *that* clause (that)	
	1 adverb clause (AC)	
	2 [main clauses]	
	4 subject-verb pairs (s v)	
	2 openers	

robin was drenched, he heartily laughed at himself,

because he knew that he looked **ridiculous**

Rewrite It! _____

Week 22

Read It! | **Mark It!** | **Fix It!** | Day 2

1 vocabulary

5 articles (ar)
6 nouns (n)
2 pronouns (pr)
1 adjective (adj)
1 adverb (adv)
1 coordinating conjunction (cc)
3 <u>prepositional phrases</u>
3 [main clauses]
3 subject-verb pairs (s v)
2 openers

2 indents
4 capitals
2 commas
2 quotations
2 end marks
1 homophone
1 apostrophe

the giant **strutted** across the log, and jokingly called

ive proven myself the better man with a laugh

robin waded too the bank

Rewrite It!

Read It!	Mark It!	Fix It!	Week 22 Day 3
1 vocabulary	1 article (ar)	1 indent	
	4 nouns (n)	2 capitals	
	3 pronouns (pr)	4 quotations	
	3 adjectives (adj)	2 end marks	
	1 prepositional phrase	1 homophone	
	1 *that* clause (that)		
	3 [main clauses]		
	4 subject-verb pairs (s v)		

give me your hand roared the stranger.

i must admit that you **wield** you're staff with

great skill

Rewrite It!

Read It!	Mark It!	Fix It!	Week 22
1 vocabulary	1 article (ar)	1 indent	Day 4
	5 nouns (n)	2 capitals	
	4 adjectives (adj)	1 comma	
	1 adverb (adv)	1 end mark	
	1 coordinating conjunction (cc)	1 number	
	2 <u>prepositional phrases</u>		
	1 *who/which* clause (w/w)		
	1 [main clause]		
	2 subject-verb pairs (s v)		
	1 opener		

robin hood then lifted his horn to his lips,

and blew 3 short blasts, which **echoed** through

the forest

Rewrite It! _____

Review It!

Who/Which Clause

A *who/which* clause adds detail to a sentence. It is a dependent clause, which means if you remove the *who/which* clause, you will still have a sentence.

Combine the two sentences by changing one into a *who/which* clause.

The outlaws distrusted the stranger. The outlaws rushed to help Robin.

_____

_____

The water flowed under the bridge. The water moved swiftly.

_____

_____

Complete the *who/which* clauses. Remember to include commas. There are multiple right answers.

Robin _____ was drenched.

The bridge _____ was just a log.

Read It!　　　　**Mark It!**　　　　**Fix It!**　　　Week 23

1 vocabulary

- 1 article (ar)
- 5 nouns (n)
- 4 adjectives (adj)
- 1 adverb (adv)
- 1 coordinating conjunction (cc)
- 2 prepositional phrases
- 3 [main clauses]
- 3 subject-verb pairs (s v)
- 2 openers

- 2 capitals
- 1 comma
- 1 end mark
- 1 homophone
- 1 number

Day 1

suddenly shouts were heard in the distance.

branches **rustled** and 20 strong outlaws burst

from there hiding places

Rewrite It!

Week 23
Day 2

Read It! | **Mark It!** | **Fix It!**

1 vocabulary

5 nouns (n)
1 pronoun (pr)
3 adjectives (adj)
1 adverb (adv)
2 prepositional phrases
1 *who/which* clause (w/w)
2 [main clauses]
3 subject-verb pairs (s v)
1 opener

1 indent
4 capitals
2 commas
2 quotations
1 end mark
1 homophone
2 apostrophes

will stutely, who was robins **steadfast** friend, immediately cried robin youre drenched from head two foot

Rewrite It! _____

Week 23

Read It!	Mark It!	Fix It!	Day 3
1 vocabulary	3 articles (ar)	1 indent	
	6 nouns (n)	4 capitals	
	4 pronouns (pr)	2 commas	
	3 adjectives (adj)	2 quotations	
	1 adverb (adv)	2 end marks	
	3 <u>prepositional phrases</u>		
	1 adverb clause (AC)		
	3 [main clauses]		
	4 subject-verb pairs (s v)		
	1 opener		

with a twinkle in his eye, robin answered i certainly am this **rugged** fellow knocked me into the water, after he gave me a beating

Rewrite It! _____

Week 23
Day 4

Read It!
- 1 vocabulary

Mark It!
- 3 articles (ar)
- 8 nouns (n)
- 4 pronouns (pr)
- 2 adjectives (adj)
- 1 adverb (adv)
- 2 prepositional phrases
- 1 who/which clause (w/w)
- 1 adverb clause (AC)
- 3 [main clauses]
- 5 subject-verb pairs (s v)
- 1 opener

Fix It!
- 2 indents
- 4 capitals
- 1 comma
- 2 quotations
- 2 end marks
- 1 homophone
- 1 number

he needs a beating himself cried will. before robin could stop them his men **pounced** on the stranger, who's strength was not a match for 20 men

Rewrite It!

Week 24

Review It!

Strong Verb, Quality Adjective, and -ly Adverb

A strong verb, a quality adjective, and an -ly adverb are three different ways to dress up writing. These stylistic devices add a strong image or feeling.

A **strong verb** is an action verb, never a linking or helping verb.

A **quality adjective** is more specific than a weak adjective. A weak adjective is overused, boring, or vague.

An **-ly adverb** is used to enhance the meaning of the verb, adjective, or adverb that it modifies.

Underline the weak word in the sentence and circle a stronger word in the list below. Think about the meaning of the words in the context of the sentence.

The outlaws ran to Robin's aid.

    fled   traveled   hopped   hurried   rushed

The hungry men ate a hearty stew.

    slurped   devoured   consumed   nibbled   feasted on

The stranger was big.

    broad   gigantic   towering   roomy   huge

Robin was a good man.

    noble   delicious   admirable   impressive   hardworking

He was awfully wet.

    very   noticeably   surprisingly   thoroughly   uncommonly

Continue to look for strong verbs, quality adjectives, and -ly adverbs in this book and write them on the collection pages found in Appendix II.

Week 24

Read It!	Mark It!	Fix It!	Day 1
1 vocabulary	2 articles (ar)	3 capitals	
	3 nouns (n)	2 commas	
	2 pronouns (pr)	2 end marks	
	1 adjective (adj)	1 apostrophe	
	2 adverbs (adv)		
	1 <u>prepositional phrase</u>		
	1 adverb clause (AC)		
	2 [main clauses]		
	3 subject-verb pairs (s v)		
	2 openers		

although the giant moved quickly robins men dragged him to the water, he **struggled** furiously

Rewrite It! _____

Week 24
Day 2

Read It!	Mark It!	Fix It!
1 vocabulary	1 article (ar)	1 indent
	3 nouns (n)	4 capitals
	2 pronouns (pr)	1 comma
	2 adjectives (adj)	2 quotations
	2 adverbs (adv)	1 end mark
	1 *that* clause (that)	1 apostrophe
	4 [main clauses]	
	5 subject-verb pairs (s v)	
	1 opener	

robin exclaimed stop! it was a fight that

he won fairly. dont harm this **blameless** man

Rewrite It! _____

_____

_____

_____

Week 24
Day 3

Read It!	**Mark It!**	**Fix It!**
1 vocabulary	2 articles (ar)	1 indent
	6 nouns (n)	4 capitals
	3 pronouns (pr)	2 commas
	2 adjectives (adj)	1 quotation
	1 adverb (adv)	1 end mark
	2 coordinating conjunctions (cc)	1 usage
	2 <u>prepositional phrases</u>
	3 [main clauses]
	3 subject-verb pairs (s v)
	1 opener

robin than bowed to the stranger, and **introduced** himself. i am the outlaw robin hood and this is my band of merry men

No closing quotation mark because quote continues.

Rewrite It! _____

Week 24 — Day 4

Read It!	**Mark It!**	**Fix It!**
1 vocabulary	2 nouns (n)	3 capitals
	8 pronouns (pr)	2 commas
	2 adjectives (adj)	1 quotation
	1 coordinating conjunction (cc)	1 end mark
	2 <u>prepositional phrases</u>	1 apostrophe
	1 adverb clause (AC)
	2 [main clauses]
	3 subject-verb pairs (s v)

No opening quotation mark because quote continues.

stranger will you stay with me and be one of us?

if youll join me i will **appoint** you my right-hand man

Rewrite It!

Week 25

Learn It!

Adjective

Week 3 you learned that an adjective describes a noun or pronoun.

Often, two or more adjectives come before a noun. The adjectives are **coordinate** if each adjective independently describes the noun that follows.

Comma

A **comma** is used to separate items in a sentence. Use a comma to separate coordinate adjectives. Because the order of coordinate adjectives is not important, the adjectives are separated with a comma.

> , Use a comma to separate coordinate adjectives.

Two tests help determine whether the adjectives before a noun are coordinate.

    Can you reverse their order?

    Can you add *and* between them?

If you answer yes, the adjectives are coordinate. Use a comma.

          adj   *adj*   *n*

They entered the untouched thick forest.

    The two adjectives *untouched* and *thick* describe the noun *forest*.

    Are they coordinate adjectives? Do they need a comma?

        Reverse the order.

            ... the thick untouched forest. Yes, you can reverse the order.

        Add *and* between the adjectives.

            ... the untouched and thick forest. Yes, you can add *and*.

          adj   *adj*   *n*

They entered the untouched**,** thick forest.

    Thick and *untouched* are coordinate adjectives and separated with a comma.

Fix It!   Add a comma between coordinate adjectives.

          adj   *adj*

Marian was a courageous**,** thoughtful maiden.

Week 25

Day 1

Read It!

1 vocabulary

Mark It!

1 article (ar)
2 nouns (n)
4 adjectives (adj)
3 adverbs (adv)
1 <u>prepositional phrase</u>
1 *who/which* clause (w/w)
1 [main clause]
2 subject-verb pairs (s v)
1 opener

Fix It!

1 indent
1 capital
1 comma
1 end mark

the stranger, who was still annoyed because of his unjust harsh **thrashing**, did not readily agree

Rewrite It! _____

Week 25

Day 2

Read It!	**Mark It!**	**Fix It!**
1 vocabulary	4 nouns (n)	3 capitals
	5 pronouns (pr)	3 commas
	6 adjectives (adj)	2 quotations
	3 adverbs (adv)	1 end mark
	1 coordinating conjunction (cc)	1 usage
	2 adverb clauses (AC)	2 apostrophes
	3 [main clauses]
	5 subject-verb pairs (s v)

can you handle your bow and arrows better

then you handle your long thick staff? if you

cant i wont join your **motley** band he retorted

Rewrite It! _____

Read It!　　　　**Mark It!**　　　　**Fix It!**　　　　Week 25

1 vocabulary

1 article (ar)　　　　1 indent
5 nouns (n)　　　　3 capitals
1 pronoun (pr)　　　2 commas
3 adjectives (adj)　　2 end marks
3 <u>prepositional phrases</u>
2 [main clauses]
2 subject-verb pairs (s v)
2 openers

Day 3

robin laughed to himself, with encouragement from his faithful **devoted** men, robin accepted the challenge

Rewrite It!

Week 25

Day 4

Read It!	Mark It!	Fix It!
1 vocabulary	2 articles (ar)	1 capital
	5 nouns (n)	2 commas
	3 pronouns (pr)	1 end mark
	4 adjectives (adj)	
	2 coordinating conjunctions (cc)	
	2 <u>prepositional phrases</u>	
	1 *that* clause (that)	
	2 [main clauses]	
	3 subject-verb pairs (s v)	
	1 opener	

he may have lost the lengthy painful **bout** with his staff but he knew that he could win a contest with his bow and arrows

Rewrite It! _____

_____

_____

_____

_____

Learn It!

Adjective

Week 3 you learned that an adjective describes a noun or pronoun.

Often, two or more adjectives come before a noun. Week 25 you learned that adjectives are **coordinate** if each adjective independently describes the noun that follows. Because the order of the coordinate adjectives is not important, the adjectives are separated with a comma.

Adjectives are **cumulative** if the first adjective describes the second adjective and the noun that follows. Cumulative adjectives follow this specific order: quantity, opinion, size, age, shape, color, origin, material, purpose.

Comma

Because cumulative adjectives must be arranged in a specific order, the adjectives are not separated with a comma.

> ✗ Do not use a comma to separate cumulative adjectives.

Two tests help determine whether the adjectives before a noun are coordinate or cumulative.

    Can you reverse their order?

    Can you add *and* between them?

If you answer yes, the adjectives are coordinate. Use a comma.
If you answer no, the adjectives are cumulative. Do not use a comma.

                     adj   *adj*   *n*
They entered the immense green forest.

    The two adjectives *immense* and *green* describe the noun *forest*.

    Are they coordinate adjectives? Do they need a comma?

        Reverse the order.

            ... the green immense forest.

        No, you cannot reverse the order: size comes before color.

        Add *and* between the adjectives.

            ... immense and green forest.

        No, you cannot add *and*.

                     adj   *adj*   *n*
They entered the immense green forest.

    Immense and *green* are cumulative adjectives and are not separated with a comma.

Fix It!   Remove the comma between cumulative adjectives.

           adj   *adj*
Marian was a brave, young maiden.

Think About It!

Adjectives can be grouped into categories. Cumulative adjectives follow this specific order: quantity, opinion, size, age, shape, color, origin, material, purpose.

Categories	Some Examples		
quantity	three	several	few
opinion	proficient	funny	smart
size	long	small	huge
age	old	young	ancient
shape	circular	curvy	square
color	red	blue	green
origin	English	African	Catholic
material	wooden	plastic	cotton
purpose	bullseye (target)	frying (pan)	baseball (glove)

Cumulative adjectives build on each other. Robin was a *skilled English* archer. He practiced with *several proficient young* men. If someone said he practiced with *young proficient several* men, your ear would tell you that was wrong. That is why the tests work. We have been trained to hear and say adjectives in a certain order, and if you try to rearrange the order of the adjectives, it sounds awkward.

Robin was a skilled English archer.

Skilled comes before *English* because *opinion* comes before *origin*.

He practiced with *several proficient young* men.

Quantity comes before *opinion*, and *opinion* comes before *age*.

They shot *long wooden* arrows.

Size comes before *material*.

They aimed at a *circular bullseye* target.

Shape comes before *purpose*.

Week 26 — Day 1

Read It!	Mark It!	Fix It!
1 vocabulary	1 article (ar)	1 indent
	8 nouns (n)	3 capitals
	4 adjectives (adj)	1 comma
	1 coordinating conjunction (cc)	1 end mark
	3 <u>prepositional phrases</u>	2 numbers
	1 *who/which* clause (which)	
	1 [main clause]	
	2 subject-verb pairs (s v)	
	1 opener	

robin **instructed** will stutely to make a target from smooth, white bark, which measured 4 fingers in height and 5 fingers in width

Rewrite It!

Week 26
Day 2

Read It!	Mark It!	Fix It!
1 vocabulary	4 articles (ar)	4 capitals
	6 nouns (n)	2 commas
	1 pronoun (pr)	2 end marks
	3 adjectives (adj)	1 usage
	2 adverbs (adv)	
	1 coordinating conjunction (cc)	
	2 <u>prepositional phrases</u>	
	2 [main clauses]	
	2 subject-verb pairs (s v)	
	2 openers	

carefully will positioned robin and the stranger

for the contest he than **paced** the distance

to a large, old, oak tree

Rewrite It! _____

Read It!	**Mark It!**	**Fix It!**	Week 26
		Day 3
1 vocabulary	4 articles (ar)	3 capitals
6 nouns (n)	2 commas
3 adjectives (adj)	1 end mark
2 prepositional phrases	1 apostrophe
1 adverb clause (AC)
1 [main clauses]
2 subject-verb pairs (s v)
1 opener

while will nailed the target to the tree the stranger chose a straight, wooden arrow from robins **quiver**

Rewrite It!

Week 26

Day 4

Read It!	**Mark It!**	**Fix It!**
1 vocabulary	2 articles (ar)	2 capitals
	5 nouns (n)	2 commas
	5 adjectives (adj)	1 end mark
	2 adverbs (adv)	1 apostrophe
	1 prepositional phrase	1 number
	1 *who/which* clause (w/w)
	1 adverb clause (AC)
	1 [main clause]
	3 subject-verb pairs (s v)
	1 opener

robins, merry men watched **attentively** as the stranger prepared to shoot at the small, white target, which will had hung 80 yards away

Rewrite It! _____

Review It!

#2 Prepositional and #5 Clausal Openers

A **#2 prepositional opener** is a sentence that begins with a prepositional phrase.

Write the pattern for a #2 prepositional opener.

_____

A **#5 clausal opener** is a sentence that begins with a www word (when, while, where, as, since, if, although, because) and contains a subject and a verb.

Write the pattern for a #5 clausal opener.

_____

Some words can begin either a #2 prepositional opener or a #5 clausal opener. Always check for a verb. If there is a verb, it is a clause. If there is not a verb, it is a prepositional phrase.

Complete the following sentences using the verbs and nouns in the list or words of your choice. Include a subject noun and verb to complete #5 clausal openers. Include a noun or article + noun to complete #2 prepositional openers. You may add other words to complete the thought.

[2] Beneath _____ Robin laughed.

[5] Because _____ he was pleased.

[2] Without _____ he seemed troubled.

[5] As _____ Robin lost his balance.

[2] Past _____ a fawn stood quietly.

[5] When _____ it was safe.

[2] Because of _____ Robin was tired.

[5] After _____ he knew it was a mistake.

Edit the above sentences by making sure the commas are inserted correctly.

Verbs
charged
fled
leaped
mocked
rushed
slipped
sprinted
trusted

Nouns
aid
apple tree
bow and arrow
bushes
cliff
competition
deer
moon
Robin
thunderstorm

Week 27

Read It! | **Mark It!** | **Fix It!** | Day 1

1 vocabulary

4 articles (ar)
4 nouns (n)
2 adverbs (adv)
1 coordinating conjunction (cc)
1 prepositional phrase
1 who/which clause (w/w)
1 [main clause]
2 subject-verb pairs (s v)
1 opener

1 capital
2 commas
1 end mark

confidently the stranger pulled the bowstring aimed at the target and **released** the arrow, which flew straight

Rewrite It! _____

Week 27

Day 2

Read It!	Mark It!	Fix It!
1 vocabulary	3 articles (ar)	2 capitals
	5 nouns (n)	2 commas
	1 pronoun (pr)	1 end mark
	4 adjectives (adj)	1 homophone
	2 <u>prepositional phrases</u>	1 apostrophe
	1 adverb clause (AC)	
	1 [main clauses]	
	2 subject-verb pairs (s v)	
	1 opener	

as it hit the center of the target robins men clapped there hands at the unexpected **impressive** shot

Rewrite It! _____

Week 27
Day 3

Read It!	**Mark It!**	**Fix It!**

1 vocabulary

2 articles (ar)
6 nouns (n)
2 pronouns (pr)
2 adjectives (adj)
2 adverbs (adv)
1 coordinating conjunction (cc)
3 prepositional phrases
3 [main clauses]
3 subject-verb pairs (s v)
3 openers

1 indent
5 capitals
2 commas
2 end marks

with care robin hood stepped to the mark,

he **notched** an arrow. playfully he winked

at his men, and boldly took his shot

Rewrite It!

Week 27 — Day 4

Read It!	Mark It!	Fix It!
1 vocabulary	1 article (ar)	2 capitals
	4 nouns (n)	2 commas
	1 pronoun (pr)	1 end mark
	2 adjectives (adj)	1 usage
	2 adverbs (adv)	2 apostrophes
	1 coordinating conjunction (cc)	
	1 <u>prepositional phrase</u>	
	1 adverb clause (AC)	
	2 [main clauses]	
	3 subject-verb pairs (s v)	
	1 opener	

robins arrow split the strangers arrow and than everyone shouted for joy, because robin had shot **flawlessly**

Rewrite It! _____

Review It!

Quotations

Quotation marks indicate words are spoken. The quote is the sentence in quotation marks. The attribution is the person speaking and the speaking verb.

Read the story below. Place quotation marks around the words that are spoken. Insert attributions. Use ideas listed in the margin or words of your choice.

Watch those two silly men, _____ A. Mama answered

_____ . They are fighting over who crosses first!

Will the tall man win? _____ B. the little bird cried

_____ .

He looks stronger, _____ C. the mama bird told her baby

_____ , but the other is quick on his feet.

Oh! _____

_____ . The smaller one   D. Mama wisely concluded

has fallen in!

Well, pride goes before a fall! _____

_____ .   E. the baby bird asked

Week 28 Day 1

Read It!

1 vocabulary

Mark It!

2 articles (ar)
6 nouns (n)
2 pronouns (pr)
4 adjectives (adj)
2 adverbs (adv)
4 [main clauses]
4 subject-verb pairs (s v)

Fix It!

1 indent
4 capitals
1 comma
4 quotations
2 end marks
1 homophone

robin i can't believe my eyes cried the stranger.

that shot was a **magnificent** shot! i will gladly join

you're band

Rewrite It!

Week 28
Day 2

Read It!
- 1 vocabulary

Mark It!
- 1 article (ar)
- 3 nouns (n)
- 5 pronouns (pr)
- 4 adjectives (adj)
- 1 adverb (adv)
- 1 coordinating conjunction (cc)
- 1 *that* clause (that)
- 4 [main clauses]
- 5 subject-verb pairs (s v)

Fix It!
- 1 indent
- 4 capitals
- 3 commas
- 2 quotations
- 1 end mark
- 1 usage

than i have gained a useful strong man and we are honored that you would join us. tell me your name robin **urged**

Rewrite It!

Week 28

Read It! — 1 vocabulary

Mark It!
- 4 nouns (n)
- 6 pronouns (pr)
- 1 adjective (adj)
- 2 adverbs (adv)
- 1 prepositional phrase
- 1 *that* clause (that)
- 1 adverb clause (AC)
- 3 [main clauses]
- 5 subject-verb pairs (s v)

Fix It!
- 1 indent
- 5 capitals
- 2 commas
- 2 quotations
- 2 end marks

Day 3

men call me john little i promise that i will serve you faithfully he proudly responded, as he **extended** his hand in friendship

Rewrite It!

Week 28

Day 4

Read It!	Mark It!	Fix It!
1 vocabulary	2 articles (ar)	1 indent
	7 nouns (n)	5 capitals
	1 pronoun (pr)	1 comma
	3 adjectives (adj)	2 quotations
	2 <u>prepositional phrases</u>	2 end marks
	1 *who/which* clause (w/w)	1 homophone
	1 adverb clause (AC)	
	3 [main clauses]	
	5 subject-verb pairs (s v)	
	1 opener	

john little is a funny name for a man whose your size **snickered** will stutely. he laughed, until tears ran down his face

Rewrite It! _____

Week 29

Review It!

Verb

An **action verb** shows action or ownership.
A **linking verb** links the subject to a noun or adjective.
A **helping verb** helps an action verb or a linking verb.

Circle the correct answers. Each statement has two correct answers.

An action verb

    a. can be a strong verb   b. is always followed by another verb

    c. always follows a helping verb   d. always expresses ownership or action

A linking verb can be followed by

    a. an action verb   b. a linking verb

    c. a noun   d. an adjective

A helping verb can be followed by

    a. an action verb   b. a linking verb

    c. a noun   d. an adjective

Circle **H** for helping or **L** for linking to identify the underlined verbs in the following sentences.

H   L   That <u>is</u> a fine shot!

H   L   That's the finest I <u>have</u> ever beheld!

H   L   Both archers <u>would</u> gladly compete at the next tournament.

H   L   Both <u>are</u> skillful.

Read It!	**Mark It!**	**Fix It!**	Week 29
			Day 1
1 vocabulary	2 articles (ar)	1 indent
	5 nouns (n)	4 capitals
	1 pronoun (pr)	2 commas
	2 adjectives (adj)	2 end marks
	3 adverbs (adv)	1 usage
	1 coordinating conjunction (cc)
	2 prepositional phrases
	1 *who/which* clause (w/w)
	2 [main clauses]
	3 subject-verb pairs (s v)
	2 openers

than robin hood, and his entire band **howled**

with delight, after a moment the stranger,

who silently watched them, slowly smiled

Rewrite It!

Week 29

Day 2

Read It!	Mark It!	Fix It!
1 vocabulary	4 articles (ar)	2 capitals
	6 nouns (n)	2 commas
	2 adjectives (adj)	1 end mark
	3 adverbs (adv)	1 homophone
	1 coordinating conjunction (cc)	
	2 <u>prepositional phrases</u>	
	4 [main clauses]	
	4 subject-verb pairs (s v)	
	2 openers	

robin laughed his men laughed and soon the stranger laughed to. merrily the forest rang with the **jubilant** noise of the men

Rewrite It! _____

Week 29 Day 3

Read It!

1 vocabulary

Mark It!

3 articles
6 nouns (n)
1 pronoun (pr)
3 adjectives (adj)
1 prepositional phrase
4 [main clauses]
4 subject-verb pairs (s v)

Fix It!

2 indents
6 capitals
4 quotations
3 end marks

little john is an ideal name for him **quipped**

will stutely. little john is the perfect name

shouted the merry men

Rewrite It! _____

_____

_____

_____

Read It! **Mark It!** **Fix It!** Week 29

Day 4

1 vocabulary
1 article (ar)
6 nouns (n)
4 pronouns (pr)
1 adjective (adj)
2 adverbs (adv)
1 coordinating conjunction (cc)
1 prepositional phrase
1 adverb clause (AC)
5 [main clauses]
6 subject-verb pairs (s v)
1 opener

1 indent
7 capitals
4 commas
2 quotations
1 end mark

at last robin said men, we can **guffaw**, until the sun sets but laughter will not feed us. join us little john. you must be hungry too

Rewrite It!

Review It!

Fill in the blanks below with different parts of speech in order to create a silly version of "Robin Hood."

After you have completed the list on this page, transfer your words to the blanks in the story on page 181.

1 adjective _____

1 noun (place) _____

1 action verb _____

1 adjective _____

1 action verb (past tense) _____

1 -ly adverb _____

1 adjective _____

1 noun _____

1 noun (time period) _____

1 noun (place) _____

1 -ly adverb _____

2 nouns _____ _____

1 noun (animal) _____

1 -ly adverb _____

1 speaking verb _____

2 adjectives _____ _____

1 adjective _____

1 -ly adverb _____

1 action verb (past tense) _____

1 -ly adverb _____

1 noun (food) _____

1 adjective _____

Week 30
Day 1

Read It!

1 vocabulary

Mark It!

2 articles (ar)
7 nouns (n)
1 pronoun (pr)
6 adjectives (adj)
1 coordinating conjunction (cc)
2 prepositional phrases
1 *who/which* clause (w/w)
1 adverb clause (AC)
1 [main clause]
3 subject-verb pairs (s v)
1 opener

Fix It!

1 indent
1 capital
2 commas
1 end mark
1 homophone
1 apostrophe

robin and his men **retraced** their steps through the ancient, green woodland, until they reached there camp, which provided safety from the kings men

Rewrite It! _____

Read It!	Mark It!	Fix It!	
1 vocabulary	3 articles (ar)	4 capitals	
	5 nouns (n)	3 commas	
	1 pronoun (pr)	2 end marks	
	2 adjectives (adj)	1 homophone	
	1 coordinating conjunction (cc)		
	2 prepositional phrases		
	1 adverb clause (AC)		
	2 [main clauses]		
	3 subject-verb pairs (s v)		
	2 openers		

after the men returned they feasted sang and danced into the evening during there **festivity** little john was the honored guest

Rewrite It! _____

Read It! | **Mark It!** | **Fix It!** | Week 30 Day 3

1 vocabulary

3 articles (ar)
4 nouns (n)
4 pronouns (pr)
1 adjective (adj)
3 adverbs (adv)
2 coordinating conjunctions (cc)
2 prepositional phrases
4 [main clauses]
4 subject-verb pairs (s v)
2 openers

2 capitals
1 comma
1 end mark

each family **warmly** welcomed him and soon he was one of them. eventually, the sun set, and the moon rose above the treetops

Rewrite It!

Week 30
Day 4

Read It!
1 vocabulary

Mark It!
2 articles (ar)
6 nouns (n)
5 adjectives (adj)
1 coordinating conjunction (cc)
4 prepositional phrases
1 [main clause]
1 subject-verb pair (s v)
1 opener

Fix It!
1 indent
5 capitals
3 commas
1 end mark
2 homophones

for many years little john lived with the merry men served as there second-in-command and proved a jolly **trustworthy** companion too robin hood

Rewrite It! _____

Word Game!

Use the words you chose on page 175 to complete the story.

Maid Marian

by _____
your name

Maid Marian, who was very _____, lived in a _____ under the
*adjective**noun (place)*

protection of King Richard. He had left the country to _____ in battle. While
action verb

the king was away, John, his _____ brother, _____ the land. Because
*adjective**action verb (past tense)*

John _____ taxed the peasants, Maid Marian was _____. She wanted
*-ly adverb**adjective*

Robin Hood's _____.
noun

One _____ Maid Marian ventured into the _____, looking for
*noun (time period)**noun (place)*

Robin Hood.

She said to him, "John's sheriff has become _____ rich by taxing the
-ly adverb

peasants. He has taken their _____ and _____. Tuesday he will
*noun**noun*

ride through the forest on a _____ to protect a wagonload of stolen goods.
noun (animal)

_____ make him return them to the poor."
-ly adverb

Robin Hood _____, "You are as _____ as you are
*speaking verb**adjective*

_____. I will follow your plan."
adjective

In this way Maid Marian helped Robin and his men return to the _____
adjective

poor what was _____ taken from them.
-ly adverb

When King Richard later returned from the wars, he _____ peace.
action verb (past tense)

Because Robin Hood was no longer an outlaw, he and Maid Marian _____ were
-ly adverb

married. They served _____ at the _____ wedding feast, and all had
*noun (food)**adjective*

a merry time!

Appendices

Appendix I: Complete Story
    Robin Hood.. 185
Appendix II: Collection Pages
    -ly Adverb 191
    Strong Verb 193
    Quality Adjective 195
Appendix III: Lists
    Pronoun... 197
    Preposition, Verb, Conjunction.. 198

Robin Hood

In the olden days of England, King Richard reigned over the land. A legendary outlaw lived in Sherwood Forest in central England. His name was Robin Hood. Robin and the loyal men with him rambled through the countryside. They hunted in the deep forests. Robin was skilled with the bow. In truth, he was the most experienced archer in England.

Why was Robin Hood an outlaw under the wrath of the law? It's an interesting story for children and adults. The sheriff of Nottingham had challenged the local archers to a shooting match and even offered a prize. Robin was just eighteen. He readily accepted the challenge, grabbed his bow, and left his hometown. Robin strolled merrily. The trip shouldn't take him more than two or three days. Robin whistled and thought about the contest, which would be entertaining. He wasn't worried about the other archers. The day seemed pleasant and carefree. However, Robin's mood would soon change.

Robin met fifteen foresters who worked for the king. They were sitting beneath a huge oak and were feasting sociably. A man who had a scar on his face confronted Robin. He called Robin's bow and arrows cheap and shoddy. Then Robin grew angry. No young man likes other men to taunt him about his prize possessions. He boasted that he was as skillful with a bow and arrow as any man. He was headed to Nottingham to prove his skill in a champion match. He planned to shoot with other archers for the grand prize, which was a barrel of exceptional ale and a new bow. One forester laughed at him and retorted that he had big words for a little boy! He said that he should drink his ale with milk.

Robin immediately took offense and challenged the forester. "Sir, do you see the deer at the edge of the wood? I bet you twenty pounds that I can hit it."

Composedly Robin took his bow in his hand, grabbed an arrow from its pouch, and drew the feather to his ear. The arrow hit the buck. The foresters seethed with rage, especially the man who lost the bet.

The loser heatedly responded, "Fool, you killed the king's deer. It's a capital offense. By law you're going to die."

In anger the forester impulsively sprang to his feet, grabbed his bow, and shot an arrow at Robin. Robin Hood was fortunate that the arrow barely missed him. Without delay the furious forester reached for a second arrow. In self-defense young Robin shot an arrow, which struck the man. He toppled forward with a cry.

Robin Hood was very upset. It tortured his conscience that he'd killed a man. Fearfully Robin Hood escaped to Sherwood Forest. He was an outlaw on two accounts and could not return home. In a single day he had shot a deer that the king reserved for his own table and had slain a man too.

The sheriff of Nottingham and the dead forester were related. Firmly he vowed that Robin must be punished. Within a few days Robin heard that a lavish reward of two hundred pounds would be given to the man who captured him.

For an entire year Robin sheltered in Sherwood Forest while he met other outlaws and gained valuable hunting skills. Eventually, he gathered a band of loyal men. These good men had been displaced for many reasons. Some men, who were famished, shot deer because they had too little food. They'd narrowly escaped from the foresters when they were hunting the king's deer. Others, who were strong and goodhearted, had lost their farms because the greedy king wanted their lands. Tragically, some had been devastated by unreasonable taxes that they couldn't pay. Throughout England poor families fled from their homes and secretly hid in Sherwood Forest. A band of forty-five brave peasants, who greatly admired Robin Hood, chose him to be their leader.

Robin's followers declared that they would rob everyone who had robbed them. Especially if powerful men plundered the poor, Robin and his men would recapture their goods and would return them. To those in need, these men would offer aid and protection. They earnestly swore that they would never harm a maid, wife, or widow. Because of the desperate times, these men, whose families were hungry, stole money from corrupt noblemen. They gave it to the peasants.

The peasants loved Robin and his merry men. They often told tales of their courageous deeds. Repeatedly Robin and his men moved their camp because they were always in peril. For entertainment the men enjoyed competitions, target practice, and fishing in the cold, gurgling brook. The children of the merry men romped along the bank. They laughed and joked together.

Although everyone seemed happy, Robin was restless. "For fourteen days we've enjoyed very little sport, my friends," he complained. "While I journey to Nottingham to seek adventures, you can wait for me here," Robin directed. He told his men that they should come quickly when they heard his signal, which would be three short blasts on his bugle.

Robin Hood roamed through the forest. He searched for adventure. At a sharp curve in a path, Robin neared a log, which spanned a broad pebbly stream and acted as a narrow bridge. As he approached the log, he noticed a large, stout stranger, who was approaching the log from the other side. Robin quickened his pace. The stranger did too. Both wanted to cross.

"Go back, sir," demanded Robin rudely. "The one who's the better man should cross first."

The confident stranger responded, "You go back. I am the better man."

Naturally, this riled Robin since his merry men always respected him and obeyed him immediately. "If you don't go back, I'll fire an arrow at you!" asserted Robin.

"Hah! Do you think that I'm afraid?" the other mocked.

"You joke like a fool!" bellowed Robin. "I could fire this arrow through your heart!"

The tall stranger chuckled, "You stand there with a lethal bow. I only carry a staff. Are you a coward?"

"I have never been called a coward!" cried Robin, whose face became crimson. "I'll teach you a lesson that you won't forget. Stay where you are! After I make a staff, I will test your sparring skills."

"I welcome you to try," countered the stranger with a twinkle in his eye. "I'm happy to wait." Patiently the calm giant leaned on his staff and waited there for Robin. He whistled as he gazed about.

Robin Hood stepped into the forest, found a tall oak, and cut a sturdy staff, which measured six feet in length. Robin fashioned his weapon. He secretly studied the giant, and he confidently planned his first move. Until that day Robin had never met a larger man. Usually, Robin towered over others. This rival was a seven-foot man! Although Robin's shoulders were broad, the stranger's shoulders were two times the size. Carefully Robin crafted his weapon, which must be strong, straight, and sturdy. He was determined that he would win. As Robin worked, he smiled, for he had found his adventure. Despite its risk Robin welcomed a challenge.

Robin Hood then goaded the giant man. "I'm ready, stranger. Fight me if you dare. When one of us falls into the stream, then the victor will be the better man."

"Ah, it's a fair test," agreed the stranger. "He who is more adept with the staff is most certainly the better man."

The giant nimbly twirled his staff above his head. It whistled through the air as Robin stepped onto the log. Quickly Robin approached his adversary on the bridge. He dodged the stranger's staff and then returned a blow to the stranger's head. Most would have tumbled into the water, but the stranger parried Robin's blow to the right. Both men began to sweat. In response the seven-foot man fiercely returned another blow. It would have easily leveled a weaker opponent. When Robin Hood deftly pushed the opponent's staff to the side, he showed him that this was no easy fight.

After an hour neither had budged an inch. Both stood where they had begun. As they battled, both men gave and received many blows until cuts and bruises covered their bodies. Each had aching muscles too. Despite fatigue neither considered quitting or seemed likely to tumble off the bridge. As the two men rested, each man privately believed that he had never met a more skillful opponent.

Although both were wounded, the battle continued. Finally, Robin delivered a mighty blow, which struck his opponent's ribs. Instantly the stranger recovered, raised his arms, and brought his staff down on Robin's head. This caused blood to flow. The jolt inflamed Robin, so he swung at the other man. The stranger ducked and avoided Robin's staff. At once the stranger counterattacked. As Robin lost his footing, he tumbled into the chilly water. Robin was drenched. He heartily laughed at himself because he knew that he looked ridiculous.

The giant strutted across the log and jokingly called, "I've proven myself the better man."

With a laugh Robin waded to the bank.

"Give me your hand!" roared the stranger. "I must admit that you wield your staff with great skill."

Robin Hood then lifted his horn to his lips and blew three short blasts, which echoed through the forest. Suddenly shouts were heard in the distance. Branches rustled, and twenty strong outlaws burst from their hiding places.

Will Stutely, who was Robin's steadfast friend, immediately cried, "Robin, you're drenched from head to foot!"

With a twinkle in his eye, Robin answered, "I certainly am. This rugged fellow knocked me into the water after he gave me a beating."

"He needs a beating himself!" cried Will.

Before Robin could stop them, his men pounced on the stranger, whose strength was not a match for twenty men. Although the giant moved quickly, Robin's men dragged him to the water. He struggled furiously.

Robin exclaimed, "Stop! It was a fight that he won fairly. Don't harm this blameless man!"

Robin then bowed to the stranger and introduced himself. "I am the outlaw Robin Hood, and this is my band of merry men. Stranger, will you stay with me and be one of us? If you'll join me, I will appoint you my right-hand man."

The stranger, who was still annoyed because of his unjust, harsh thrashing, did not readily agree. "Can you handle your bow and arrows better than you handle your long, thick staff? If you can't, I won't join your motley band," he retorted.

Robin laughed to himself. With encouragement from his faithful, devoted men, Robin accepted the challenge. He may have lost the lengthy, painful bout with his staff, but he knew that he could win a contest with his bow and arrows.

Robin instructed Will Stutely to make a target from smooth white bark, which measured four fingers in height and five fingers in width. Carefully Will positioned Robin and the stranger for the contest. He then paced the distance to a large old oak tree. While Will nailed the target to the tree, the stranger chose a straight wooden arrow from Robin's quiver. Robin's merry men watched attentively as the stranger prepared to shoot at the small white target, which Will had hung eighty yards away. Confidently the stranger pulled the bowstring, aimed at the target, and released the arrow, which flew straight. As it hit the center of the target, Robin's men clapped their hands at the unexpected, impressive shot.

With care Robin Hood stepped to the mark. He notched an arrow. Playfully he winked at his men and boldly took his shot. Robin's arrow split the stranger's arrow, and then everyone shouted for joy because Robin had shot flawlessly.

"Robin, I can't believe my eyes!" cried the stranger. "That shot was a magnificent shot! I will gladly join your band."

"Then I have gained a useful, strong man, and we are honored that you would join us. Tell me your name," Robin urged.

"Men call me John Little. I promise that I will serve you faithfully," he proudly responded as he extended his hand in friendship.

"John Little is a funny name for a man who's your size!" snickered Will Stutely. He laughed until tears ran down his face.

Then Robin Hood and his entire band howled with delight. After a moment the stranger, who silently watched them, slowly smiled. Robin laughed, his men laughed, and soon the stranger laughed too. Merrily the forest rang with the jubilant noise of the men.

"Little John is an ideal name for him!" quipped Will Stutely.

"Little John is the perfect name!" shouted the merry men.

At last Robin said, "Men, we can guffaw until the sun sets, but laughter will not feed us. Join us, Little John. You must be hungry too."

Robin and his men retraced their steps through the ancient green woodland until they reached their camp, which provided safety from the king's men. After the men returned, they feasted, sang, and danced into the evening. During their festivity Little John was the honored guest. Each family warmly welcomed him, and soon he was one of them. Eventually, the sun set, and the moon rose above the treetops.

For many years Little John lived with the merry men, served as their second-in-command, and proved a jolly, trustworthy companion to Robin Hood.

-ly Adverb
An **-ly adverb** dresses up writing because it creates a strong image or feeling.

Strong Verb

A **strong verb** dresses up writing because it creates a strong image or feeling. A strong verb is an action verb, never a linking or helping verb.

Quality Adjective

A **quality adjective** dresses up writing because it creates a strong image or feeling. A quality adjective is more specific than a weak adjective, which is overused, boring, or vague.

Pronoun

A **pronoun** replaces a noun in order to avoid repetition.

A **personal pronoun** takes the place of common and proper nouns. It should agree with its antecedent in number, person, and case.

A **reflexive pronoun** ends in -self or -selves and refers to the subject of the same sentence.

2 numbers	3 persons	**Subjective** function as — subject, subject complement	**Objective** function as — object of a preposition, direct object, indirect object	**Possessive** function as — adjective	**Possessive** function as — pronoun	**Reflexive** refers to — subject of same sentence
singular	1st	I	me	my	mine	myself
singular	2nd	you	you	your	yours	yourself
singular	3rd	he, she, it	him, her, it	his, her, its	his, hers, its	himself, herself, itself
plural	1st	we	us	our	ours	ourselves
plural	2nd	you	you	your	yours	yourselves
plural	3rd	they	them	their	theirs	themselves

A **relative pronoun** begins a dependent *who/which* clause. The pronoun *who* has three forms: *who* (subjective), *whom* (objective), *whose* (possessive).

who, whom, whose, which, that

An **interrogative pronoun** is used to ask a question.

what, whatever, which, whichever, who, whoever, whom, whose

A **demonstrative pronoun** points to a particular person or thing. When a word on the demonstrative list is placed before a noun, it functions as an adjective, not a pronoun.

this, that, these, those

An **indefinite pronoun** is not definite. It does not refer to any particular person or thing. When a word on the indefinite list is placed before a noun, it functions as an adjective, not a pronoun.

Singular and Plural	Plural	Singular				
all	both		each	much	one	
any	few	another	either	neither	other	
more	many	anybody	everybody	nobody	somebody	
most	others	anyone	everyone	no one	someone	
none	own	anything	everything	nothing	something	
some	several	anywhere	everywhere	nowhere	somewhere	

Preposition

A **preposition** starts a phrase that shows the relationship between a noun or pronoun and another word in the sentence. **PATTERN preposition + noun (no verb)**

This is not an exhaustive list. When in doubt, consult a dictionary.

aboard	amid	beneath	down	into	opposite	throughout	up
about	among	beside	during	like	out	to	upon
above	around	besides	except	minus	outside	toward	with
according to	as	between	for	near	over	under	within
across	at	beyond	from	of	past	underneath	without
after	because of	by	in	off	regarding	unlike	
against	before	concerning	inside	on	since	until	
along	behind	despite	instead of	onto	through	unto	

Verb

A **verb** shows action, links the subject to another word, or helps another verb.

An **action verb** shows action or ownership.

A **linking verb** links the subject to a noun or adjective.
 am, is, are, was, were, be, being, been (be verbs)
 seem, become, appear, grow, remain, taste, sound, smell, feel, look (verbs dealing with the senses)

A **helping verb** helps an action verb or a linking verb.
 am, is, are, was, were, be, being, been (be verbs)
 have, has, had, do, does, did, may, might, must, can, will, shall, could, would, should

Conjunction

A **conjunction** connects words, phrases, or clauses.

An **coordinating conjunction** (cc) connects the same type of words, phrases, or clauses.
 FANBOYS   for, and, nor, but, or, yet, so

A **subordinating conjunction** (www word) connects an adverb clause to a main clause.
 www.asia.b   when, while, where, as, since, if although, because
     before, after, until, unless, whenever, whereas, than

FIX-L3-S
ISBN 978-1-62341-361-3